MARGUERITE PATTEN

SECOND PICCOLO
COOK BOOK

By the same author in Piccolo
PICCOLO COOK BOOK

MARGUERITE PATTEN

SECOND PICCOLO COOK BOOK

Illustrations by Eileen Strange

A Piccolo Original
Pan Books Ltd
London and Sydney

First published 1973 by Pan Books Ltd,
Cavaye Place, London SW10 9PG

ISBN 0 330 23715 2

2nd Printing 1974
3rd Printing 1974

© Marguerite Patten 1973

Printed in Great Britain by
Cox &Wyman Ltd, London, Reading and Fakenham

CONTENTS

INTRODUCTION

Here is another cookery book to follow the first *Piccolo Cook Book*.* The recipes are quite different, but they are still planned so you can cook them yourselves, without any trouble. They are easy, not too expensive, and very good to eat.

This book will help you to cook:

Supper dishes and snacks: some of them can be prepared in just a few minutes.
A complete dinner: with hints to make it easy to do.
Interesting puddings and desserts: including home-made ice cream and lots of ideas using ice cream.
Cakes, buns and biscuits: of all kinds.

Please read the first few pages before you begin cooking; they remind you of the special words and tools used in cookery and they also tell you about the work food does in keeping us strong and healthy.

I hope you like these recipes. Follow the instructions carefully: if anything is in capitals or in italics in a recipe, it means it is especially important. I have not reminded you about warming plates and dishes in every recipe, but this is important too.
USE OVEN GLOVES OR AN OVEN CLOTH TO
HOLD HOT DISHES

Good luck and good cooking!   Marguerite Patten

*Originally published as *Junior Cook Book*.

SOME TOOLS YOU WILL USE

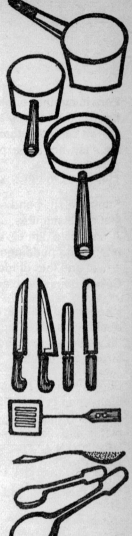

Your hands are important 'tools' in cooking, so wash them well before you handle food.

Here are some of the tools mentioned in recipes:

Frying pans and saucepans: make sure you choose them large enough for the amount of food. If you have non-stick pans ask a grown-up how to take care of them.

Knives: you will use several different kinds of knives when you cook. You will need a sharp knife for cutting and chopping – ALWAYS BE VERY CAREFUL HOW YOU USE A SHARP KNIFE. Ask a grown-up to help you chop difficult things. If you have a chopping board, cut on this, so that you do not mark the table. Cut bread with a bread knife on a bread or chopping board. Spread butter on bread with a flat-bladed knife; a pointed knife makes holes in the bread. Lift food out of pans with a wide-bladed knife called a palette knife, or use a fish slice, that looks like this.

Spoons: when you stir use a wooden spoon; but when you measure use the type of spoon mentioned in the recipe.

ALWAYS HAVE just enough food to give a LEVEL spoon measure. If you over-fill the spoon you will have too much for the recipe.

Scales: if you have no scales a grown-up will help you work out the amounts. Today some people use metric measures (grammes and kilograms), others use Imperial measures (ounces and pounds). This book gives you both: metric measures come first and Imperial follow in brackets immediately afterwards, so that you can choose which to follow.

Measures: if you have a proper measuring jug use this; if not, remember that a teacup holds about 142 ml ($\frac{1}{4}$ pint) and a breakfast cup about 284 ml ($\frac{1}{2}$ pint). Many recipes give spoon measures. Always fill the spoon so that it is LEVEL, not more.

A grater: is used for making pieces of cheese, lemon rind, etc, smaller. If you rub a slice of bread against the coarse side of the grater you make breadcrumbs. The picture shows the most usual kind.

A colander: is used for straining vegetables.

A pastry brush: is used for many things including greasing baking tins and dishes. Take a very little margarine or fat from the amount mentioned in the recipe, warm it and brush over the dish, or rub the unmelted fat over the tin or dish with greaseproof paper.

Serving dishes: sometimes the recipe just says use a serving dish, which means any kind of dish from the cupboard. In other recipes you are told to use an *oven-proof* dish: this means it is made of something like Pyrex which can be put into the oven but must not go on top of the cooker or under the grill. In other recipes you are told to use a *heat-proof* (and some books call it a flame-proof) dish; this means the kind of special dish like Pyrosil or heat-proof Wedgwood that can go under the grill or in the oven or on top of the cooker.

An egg whisk or *rotary whisk:* is used to whip cream, beat up egg white, etc.

Cake tins: there are many sorts of cake tins, but for the recipes in this book you will need a baking tray, patty tins, paper cake cases, and a sandwich tin.

Basins and bowls: you will need a nice big mixing bowl (never try to mix a recipe in too small a bowl: it is very difficult!) and some smaller basins for whisking egg, whipping cream, and so on.

Sieves: for straining liquids. Use small ones for tea or coffee, and larger ones where there is more liquid. You also need a sieve to make sure there are no lumps in flour.

WORDS USED IN COOKING

Mixing

BEATING: means mixing the ingredients together with a very brisk movement. A wooden spoon is generally used.

BLENDING: also means mixing the ingredients together.

CREAMING: means beating fat and sugar together until they are soft and fluffy; use a wooden spoon.

FOLDING: is a turning movement done gently and slowly with a metal spoon, as in the Orange Alaska (pages 146–147)

KNEADING: means mixing the ingredients firmly together with your hands, as in the Home-made bread (pages 101–109) and Rolls and Buns (pages 110–117).

RUBBING IN: is a method of mixing fat with flour with the tips of your fingers; you do this in the Cherry tarts (pages 132–136) and a lot of other recipes in this book.

WHISKING: is a very brisk movement to whip cream or egg whites and is done by hand or with a rotary whisk.

Cooking

BAKING: is the method of cooking food in the oven, such as cakes.

BOILING: is cooking in liquid at boiling point (100°C or 212°F), as in boiling cauliflower (page 93, stage 27).

FRYING: is cooking in fat; *do be careful* when you do this. Page 82 tells you about testing the temperature of the fat.

GRILLING: is cooking under the grill in a quick heat.

SIMMERING: is steady cooking in liquid. You should see an occasional bubble on the surface.

WARMING: hot foods should be served on hot plates or dishes. Heat these on racks on the top of the cooker, in the warming compartment or in the oven set very low.

SYMBOLS USED IN THIS BOOK

This means you will need to light the gas oven or switch on the electric oven. Your mother may prefer to do this for you. If you have a solid-fuel oven ask a grown-up how to use it.

This symbol is for the grill, and shows that you will need to use it.

This shows that you use the top of the cooker. Ask your mother to explain how to turn down the burner or hotplate during cooking.

This means you need to weigh the food on scales. This book gives both metric weights (grammes and kilograms) and Imperial weights (oz and lb) – see pages 14 and 15.

THE METRIC SYSTEM

In Britain we have always used Imperial weights and measures, but in the future we shall be using metric weights and measures. In order to help you become familiar with the metric system and learn to compare it with the Imperial one, you will find that all recipes have both side by side. If one tries to give the *exact* grammes to correspond to the *exact* Imperial measure, it often is a very complicated amount. This is why you will find that in this, and many other books, an approximate weight or measure is suggested.

Imperial weight	Metric weight	
	Exact grammes and kilos	Approx
1 oz	28·35	25
2 oz	56·7	50
3 oz	85·05	75
4 oz	113·4	100
8 oz	226·8	200
1 lb	453·6	½ kilo (poor weight)
2 lb	907·2	1 kilo (poor weight)

As you will see, the approximate amount is *less* than the real amount, so that you will produce slightly *less* mixture with the metric mixtures than with the Imperial ones.

Imperial measure	Metric measure Exact ml*	Approx litre** (always be generous with your measure)
¼ pint	142	⅛
½ pint	284	¼
¾ pint	426	⅜
1 pint	568	½
1¼ pints	710	⅝
1½ pints	852	¾
1¾ pints	994	⅞
2 pints	1136	1

*1000 millilitres (ml)=1 litre.
**½ litre = ·88 pints
 1 litre = 1·76 pints.

In addition to changes in weight and liquid measures we shall be using metric measures of length – e.g. cake tins in the future will be marked in centimetres and not in inches.

Imperial length	Metric length Exact cm	Approx cm
1 inch	2·54	2
2 inches	5·08	5
4 inches	10·16	10
6 inches	15·24	15
8 inches	20·32	20
10 inches	25·40	25

Oven temperatures will be in Celcius (°C) instead of Fahrenheit (°F).

Imperial temperature °F	Metric temperature	
	Exact °C	Approx °C
200	93	90
225	107	110
250	121	130
275	135	140
300	149	150
325	163	170
350	177	180
375	190	190
400	204	200
425	218	220
450	232	230
475	246	240

SAFETY FIRST

When you are cooking you will be handling hot food and very hot pans, as well as putting food into a heated oven or removing hot dishes from the oven.

You also will be chopping, cutting and doing other jobs that could cause accidents if you are not careful.
Here are some of the things you should remember:

ALWAYS keep saucepan or frying-pan handles turned towards the middle of the cooker for, if they stick out, you or someone else could knock against the handle and tip the pan over. When you remove pans from the cooker, take care they do not harm working surfaces: put them on a mat or pan stand.

ALWAYS let a pan containing hot fat cool down before you move it from the top of the cooker. And NEVER lean over a pan of hot fat in case some splashes on to your face or hands.

ALWAYS use oven gloves or a thick oven cloth for removing dishes from the oven. If it is a large or heavy dish, or if it is very hot, ALWAYS ask a grown-up to remove it from the oven for you.

17

None of the recipes in this book will spoil if the oven is not heated first so, if there is no one to help you with the oven, it is wiser to put the dish in the COLD oven, and then light it or switch it on to the setting or temperature given in the recipe. But NEVER do this unless you have been given permission by a grown-up and been shown exactly how to do it.

ALWAYS check that you have turned or switched off the heat from every part of the cooker when you have finished cooking.

IF ANYONE does burn their hand on a hot dish put it into cold water AT ONCE, then tell a grown-up so they may see if it needs any treatment.

Young children must NEVER USE SHARP KNIVES; grown-ups will do most of the chopping for you, I am sure. Cut food on a chopping board so that you do not harm the working surfaces.

IF YOU SPILL anything on the floor, particularly grease or something sticky, wipe it up at once so that no one will slip and hurt themselves.

Be proud of your good cooking and be equally proud that you do not cause accidents.

18

GOOD SHOPPING

I expect there are times when you shop for food. Here are some points to watch:

While waiting to be served work out just what you should pay for the food you buy, then you can check your change.

When you buy things in a supermarket check that food is carefully wrapped. Some foods are dated – bacon, for example. Make sure the date has not passed.

When you buy meat make sure it does not look dry and there is not *too much* fat; there should be *some* firm white fat on beef, firm cream fat on lamb or mutton and pinky-white fat on pork.

When you buy frozen foods carry them home as soon as possible so that they stay frozen. When you get home put them into the freezing part of the refrigerator or wrap them in newspaper to keep them frozen.

When you buy green vegetables make quite sure they look fresh; stale sprouts, cabbage or cauliflower have yellow leaves instead of fresh green leaves.

PUTTING THE FOOD AWAY

When you come home after shopping and are asked to unpack the food these are some of the things to remember:

Put ice cream or other frozen foods in the coolest place possible, that is, in the freezing compartment of the refrigerator or in the deep freeze or wrapped in newspaper in a cool cupboard.

Butter and other fats should be put into the special container in the refrigerator or into a cool cupboard.

Bread must be put into your special bread bin, drawer or other container.

Green vegetables should be taken out of their wrappings and put in a cool place; the more air they have the better they keep.

Fish and meat should be taken out of their wrappings, put on plates and placed in the refrigerator or the coolest part of the larder or ventilated cupboard.

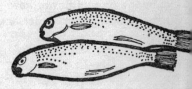

THE WORK OF FOOD

Most of us enjoy nice food and
interesting dishes, but it is
important that we also try to choose foods
that are *good* for us, as well as being
pleasant to eat.

Perhaps you do not know just what kinds
of food are important to eat, so the
following pages will tell you about some
of these.
On page 23 are suggestions for the kind
of food we should try to eat every day,
and below are the names of some of the
most important words in health-giving
foods.

PROTEINS are found in all meat,
chicken and other poultry, fish, cheese,
eggs, milk, peas, beans and lentils.
Page 24 tells you about the work of
proteins.

STARCH is found in flour and anything made with flour (such as bread, cakes, spaghetti and other pasta). It is also in some vegetables like potatoes and peas. Pages 25 and 28 tell you more about this.

SUGAR is found in sugar itself, in honey and treacle, and in things made with sugar like jam. Sugar is one of the foods that should be eaten in small quantities (see pages 25 and 28).

FATS are found in butter, margarine and other fats, and in meat and some fish (like herrings). Page 28 tells you why you need some fat.

VITAMINS are found in lots of food and pages 27 and 28 tell you about them.

Foods to eat each day

The circle shows the groups of food we
should try to eat each day, together with
the names of some of the different
products we can choose from.
In addition most people will eat some
kind of sugar and sweetening each day.
Pages 24 to 28 tell you more about the
work of the different foods.

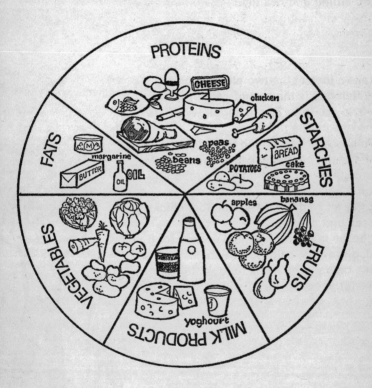

How to be strong and healthy

Most of us want to be really strong and healthy and the foods we call proteins help us a great deal in this.

When you are young and growing you MUST have proteins to build strong bones and bodies. When you have finished growing you still NEED proteins to keep you strong and healthy.

Take a look at the two pictures below. Which one is the sort of person you would like to be? I am sure it would be the one on the right.
This is why it is foolish to fill up on lots of sweets, buns and cakes and not eat enough of the protein foods first and foremost.
Enjoy all kinds of meat, fish too, chicken, eggs and cheese.
Cheese is a rather special protein for it also provides calcium, which, as you will see on page 26, helps to look after the health of our teeth.

How to be slim

Often children and grown-ups are over-weight because they eat the **wrong** foods NOT because they eat a lot of food.

Let us suppose you are rather fat.
Perhaps it is because you do not take enough exercise, in which case you will soon slim down if you walk more or play more games.
Perhaps it is because you are a NIBBLER!!! or you eat too many starchy or sweet foods.
Just think what you eat between meals.
Do you have lots of buns, cakes, lollies, ice cream and fruit squash?
This is probably the reason you are over-weight. So all you need to do is to CHANGE these rather bad habits.
Eat an apple or a raw carrot or piece of celery between meals and notice the difference.
When it comes to meal times choose plates 3 and 4 instead of plates 1 and 2.

Plate 1
sausages with heaps of chips.

Plate 2
a 'gooey' looking steamed pudding.

Plate 3
sausages, a very few chips, tomato and sprouts or cauliflower.

Plate 4
fruit salad.

How to have strong teeth

When people smile and show lovely strong white teeth it makes such a difference to their appearance, doesn't it? Many things help to give us good teeth:
Regular visits to the dentist.
Regular brushing after meals.
NOT TOO MUCH SWEET FOOD OR SOFT FOOD – we should give our teeth and gums plenty of work to do by eating crisp apples, celery, and other foods that need biting and crunching. Eat the right foods – and milk and cheese are the most important foods to help produce strong teeth. If you have plenty of these foods, end your meals with a piece of apple, **do not eat too many sweet things** and brush your teeth regularly, you should look like the bottom picture and never like the top one.

How to have a clear skin

No one likes to have spots, do they? Often spots are just a sign of growing up and will soon vanish as you become older, particularly if you are careful to keep your skin very clean.

Sometimes spots appear because people eat the wrong foods. Too many sweets and too much fried food, like chips with most meals, help to produce spots.

There is a vitamin – known as Vitamin C – that helps us to keep a clear skin, as well as shining hair and clear eyes.

Vitamin C is found in many fruits.

Vitamin C is also present in lots of vegetables:

green vegetables (they must be eaten raw or lightly cooked), potatoes (although potatoes are a starchy vegetable they also give us some Vitamin C, particularly if you eat them when new and if you eat the skins, as in jacket potatoes), and tomatoes – and have these raw whenever possible.
Vitamin C is often called the protective vitamin, for in addition to looking after our skin, eyes and hair it helps to prevent us catching a cold.

How to have lots of energy

Just think of all the things there are to do in a day. Our sketches show some of them.

In order to enjoy doing these things, as well as many others, you must have plenty of energy. Regular exercise and fresh air, the right amount of sleep and the right foods all help.

What are the right foods for energy?

We must have proteins – see pages 21, 23 and 24.
We need a certain amount of fat.
We need some starch, preferably in the form of bread, for this contains another important group of Vitamins, called Vitamin B group and they help so much to make us energetic.
We need a little sugar – but **not too much.**
We must have fruit and vegetables, for no one feels energetic if they have a bad cold and page 27 points out that the Vitamin C in fruit and vegetables helps to prevent us catching cold.
In other words, if you want to be really energetic you need a variety of foods; the recipes in this book will help to provide these in an interesting way.

SNACKS AND QUICK SUPPER DISHES

The recipes on the following pages are suitable for supper and for lunchtime snacks (if you have a main meal at night), or they could form part of a substantial tea.

The first recipes, on pages 30 to 44, are made with foods that you will find in most store cupboards. For example, sweet or savoury pancakes make a splendid snack.

The next snacks, on pages 45 to 58, are particularly quick; among these you will find milk drinks, for milk is a food as well as a beverage.

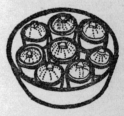

Perhaps you are planning to entertain some friends. You may enjoy making a quick supper dish or snack for them and you can find some rather more special recipes of this sort on pages 59 to 81.

Take time to make your snack look attractive; you can, for instance, garnish it with parsley or tomato.

Pancakes

Home-made pancakes can be served as a pudding or a savoury dish. Either way, they are delicious. The batter is very easy to make. Read the instructions on page 155 about the importance of looking after hot frying pans.

Pancakes with lemon

You will need:

flour (preferably plain)	100 grammes (4 oz)
salt	pinch
egg	1
milk or a mixture of milk and water	good $\frac{1}{4}$ litre (284 ml) or $\frac{1}{2}$ pint
for frying:	
fat	50 grammes (2 oz)
for serving:	
castor sugar	25 grammes (1 oz)
lemon	1

These ingredients will make 8 pancakes.

You will use:

plates for ingredients, sieve, large basin, cup or small basin, measuring jug, wooden spoon or whisk, 18–20 cm (7–8 inch) frying pan, flat knife, jug, palette knife or fish slice, oven-proof serving plate, greaseproof paper, sharp knife, chopping board, sugar dredger.

For success:

Whisk the pancake batter just before cooking.

Make sure the fat is really hot before cooking each pancake.

Pour only a very little batter into the pan so you have thin pancakes.

1 If you want to keep the pancakes hot in the oven set this to very slow, 275°F, 140°C or Gas Mark 1. If you prefer keeping them hot on top of the cooker, half fill a large saucepan with water and heat it.

2 Sieve the flour and salt into a large basin.

3 Break the egg into a cup or small basin and pour it into the flour.

4 Add about ¼ of the milk and stir carefully with a wooden spoon until the flour is blended with the egg and milk.

5 Beat really hard with the wooden spoon until you have a thick smooth mixture. It is now called a thick batter.

6 Some people like to let the thick batter stand before adding the rest of the liquid; others add the liquid straight away. Whichever method you use, pour the rest of the ¼ litre or ½ pint of liquid into the thick batter very slowly, beating all the time so that it does not become lumpy. When the liquid has nearly all been put in, you may like to change the wooden spoon for a whisk. It is important to beat really well so that the batter is nice and light. When you've beaten enough, bubbles should rise to the top of the mixture.

7 When all the liquid has been added, let the batter stand in a cool place until you are ready to use it.

8 Light the gas burner or switch on the electric hotplate.

9 Divide the fat into 8 pieces. Put one piece into the frying pan and heat steadily until melted. You will need 1 piece of fat for cooking each pancake.

10 Transfer the batter to a jug and pour enough into the hot fat to give a very thin coating.

11 TILT THE PAN AS SHOWN IN THE PICTURE SO THAT THE BATTER RUNS EVENLY OVER THE PAN. It will probably be better for a grown-up to do this first to show you the best way.

12 Cook the pancake for 2 minutes over a medium heat, then turn with the help of the palette knife or fish slice.

13 Cook for the same time on the second side, then lift on to the serving plate. The pancake should look a nice golden brown on both sides.

14 Either put into the very cool oven to keep hot or get a grown-up to lift the plate on to the pan of very hot water.

15 Continue cooking the pancakes as stages 8–13 until all are ready.

16 Sprinkle the sugar over the greaseproof paper.

17 Take the pancakes off the plate and roll neatly on the sugared paper. Be careful not to burn your fingers as you do this for they are hot.

18 Cut the lemon into slices.

19 Lift the pancakes back on to the serving plate and serve with slices of lemon.

Note: If you are having an informal meal, make one pancake and serve it at once, rolled up, with sugar and lemon. Make the second pancake and continue like this. It saves all the bother of keeping the pancakes hot.

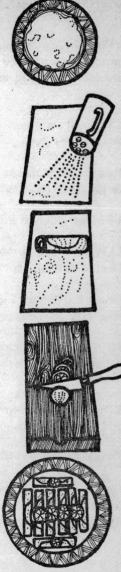

Jam pancakes

1 You will use the same mixture for the pancakes as page 30 and cook these in the same way; you will not need the lemon.

2 You will also need about 4–6 tablespoons jam.

3 Cook the pancakes as directed on pages 30–33 and keep them hot.

4 Put the jam into a saucepan.

5 Light the gas burner or switch on the electric hotplate, set to a very low heat.

6 Heat the jam for 2–3 minutes only, then take it off the heat.

7 Tip the first pancake on to the sugared paper, spread with a little warm jam and roll up neatly.

8 Do the same thing with all the pancakes and serve at once.

To make a change:

Fruit Pancakes: Open a can of fruit pie filling. Heat this in a saucepan and use it instead of jam.

Tomato pancakes

1 You will use the same mixture for the pancakes as page 30 and cook them in the same way. You will not need the sugar or lemon.

It is a good idea to prepare the tomato filling BEFORE cooking the pancakes, and for this **you will need**:

bacon	3 rashers
tomatoes	**small** can
salt	very small pinch
pepper	shake

to garnish:
parsley   small sprig

2 Cut away the bacon rinds and chop the bacon into small pieces with kitchen scissors or a sharp knife on a chopping board.

3 Light the gas burner or switch on the electric hotplate.

4 Put the bacon rinds and the pieces of bacon into a small saucepan or frying pan and fry for 3 minutes.

5 Take the pan off the heat and lift out the bacon rinds. (You added these to give more fat; you can discard them now.)

6 Open the can of tomatoes, or ask a grown-up to do this for you, and tip the tomatoes and the liquid from the can into the saucepan with the bacon. Chop the tomatoes into smaller pieces with a knife and fork. You can do this in the saucepan.

7 Add a very small pinch of salt, because most bacon is fairly salty anyway, and a shake of pepper.

8 Put the tomato mixture back on top of the cooker but do not heat again until nearly all the pancakes are cooked.

9 Cook the pancakes as instructed on pages 30–33 and keep them hot.

10 Heat the tomato mixture for a few minutes only.

11 Put the first pancake on to a hot serving dish, top with some of the tomato mixture, then add a second pancake, more tomato mixture and continue like this until you have used all the pancakes and all the tomato mixture.

12 Top with the parsley. To serve, cut these pancakes into slices, like a cake.

Eggs Mornay

When you read the word 'Mornay' you
will know the food is served with a
cheese sauce. This recipe makes a very
good supper dish. Make sure you use a
dish that can be put under the grill to
brown. Incidentally, when the mixture is
browned, it is called *au gratin*.

You will need:

eggs	4

for the sauce:

cheese	50 grammes (2 oz)
flour	25 grammes (1 oz)
salt	pinch
pepper	shake
milk	¼ litre (284 ml) or ½ pint
butter or margarine	25 grammes (1 oz)

for the topping:

grated cheese	25 grammes (1 oz)
breadcrumbs	2 tablespoons

to garnish:

tomatoes	2

These ingredients will make 4 servings.

You will use:

plates for ingredients, 2 saucepans, 2
basins, tablespoon, grater, wooden
spoon, measuring jug, knife, heat-proof
serving dish, chopping board.

For success:

Stir the sauce carefully at stage 13 so it
keeps smooth.

Do not cook the sauce when you have
put in the cheese, otherwise the mixture
becomes 'lumpy' – the proper word for
this is 'curdling'.

1 Put enough cold water into a saucepan
to cover the eggs.

2 Carry the eggs to the cooker in a basin.
Lower them into the cold water with a
tablespoon and put the saucepan over
the burner or hotplate.

3 Light the gas burner or switch on the
electric hotplate.

4 Bring the egg water to the boil, then
adjust the heat so that it isn't bubbling
too fiercely. Look at your watch or a
clock and allow the eggs to boil for 10
minutes – no longer.

5 Lift the eggs out of the water and put them into a basin of cold water.

6 When you can touch the eggs, lift them out and crack the shells; this makes sure the eggs cool quickly.

7 While the eggs are boiling you can start to prepare the sauce.

8 Grate the cheese on to a plate; you can also grate the cheese for the topping and put this on to a second plate.

9 Mix the flour with the salt and pepper in a basin.

10 Gradually add a quarter of the milk, stirring with a wooden spoon until you have a smooth paste.

11 Put the rest of the milk into a saucepan and bring to boiling point. Take care it does not boil over.

12 Pour the boiling milk slowly over the flour mixture, stirring all the time to prevent lumps forming.

13 Tip the sauce back into the pan and put over a **low** heat. Stir until the mixture boils. Then continue boiling for 3 minutes, stirring all the time. Add the butter or margarine.

14 When stirring the sauce, make sure that the wooden spoon scrapes across the bottom and into the corners of the pan. If the sauce becomes a little lumpy, remove pan from the heat, beat the sauce with the wooden spoon, or better still with a hand whisk, until it becomes smooth.

15 Add the cheese, stir to melt the cheese but do not cook the sauce again.

16 Take the shells off the eggs, then put the shelled eggs on to a plate and cut into halves.

17 Put the eggs into the heat-proof dish.

18 Light the gas grill or switch on the electric grill.

19 Pour the hot cheese sauce over the eggs.

20 Sprinkle the grated cheese and breadcrumbs over the top of the sauce.

21 Carry to the cooker and put under the grill and cook for about 4 minutes, until the top is really brown and crisp.

22 Lift the dish from under the grill **very** carefully. You will need oven gloves.

23 Cut the two tomatoes into halves and put on top of the dish and serve at once.

A cheese sauce can be used in many ways. The first *Piccolo Cook Book* gives you two recipes using this, on pages 68–73.

To make a change:

If you have any cooked spinach left you can put this in the dish at stage 17 and lay the halved eggs on top. The recipe is then called **Eggs Florentine**.

Tulip cups

These are like small tarts but save you the trouble of making pastry. In this recipe they are filled with baked beans but you can cook tomatoes or other foods in them (see page 44), or fill them with jam or fruit to serve for a dessert or for tea.

You will need:

bread	8–9 thin slices from a small fresh loaf
butter or margarine	40 grammes (1½ oz)
baked beans	medium can

These ingredients will make 8–9 cups.

You will use:

bread knife, bread board (unless using ready sliced bread), plate, rolling pin, flat-bladed knife, patty (bun) tins, can opener, saucepan, wooden spoon, serving plate, tablespoon.

For success:

Use fresh bread and roll it at stage 4. Make sure the oven is really hot.

1 Set your oven to moderately hot to hot, 400–425°F, 200–220°C or Gas Mark 5–6.

2 Slice the bread (unless using ready sliced bread) or ask a grown-up to do this for you; there is no need to cut off the crusts.

3 Put the butter or margarine on a plate and leave it in a warm place to soften slightly.

4 Roll the bread with the rolling pin on a dry working surface. This makes it easy to handle and it will not break when you put it into the patty (bun) tins.

5 Spread one side of the bread with some of the butter or margarine.

6 Press the greased side of the bread into the patty (bun) tins to get a shape as shown in the picture.

7 Spread inside the bread shapes with the rest of the butter or margarine.

8 Bake for 10 minutes towards the top of a moderately hot to hot oven until crisp and golden brown.

9 Meanwhile, open the can of beans or ask a grown-up to do this for you.

10 Tip the beans and sauce from the can into the saucepan.

11 Light the gas burner or switch on the electric hotplate.

12 Heat the beans gently for a few minutes, stirring with a wooden spoon so that they do not burn.

13 Take the tulip cups out of the oven, lift them very carefully out of the patty (bun) tins and put them on the serving plate.

14 Fill each one with the hot beans and serve at once.

To make a change:

Fill the tulip cups with:
Scrambled egg (see page 48) or scrambled egg and cheese.

Mashed sardines and slices of tomato.

Cooked tomatoes, topped with grated cheese.

Or with sweet fillings:
Jam, honey, marmalade or lemon curd.

Cooked or canned fruit, well drained.

Let the tulip cups get cold and fill with ice cream and decorate with grated chocolate.

Snacks on toast

These are very quick to prepare. The first *Piccolo Cook Book* gives you some suggestions, and here (up to page 51) are some more.

Toast 4 slices of bread, spread with butter or margarine, then spread with one of the following:

(*All quantities will cover the 4 slices.*)

Cheese and ham: Blend 100 grammes (4 oz) cream cheese with 50 grammes (2 oz) chopped cooked ham and 1 tablespoon chutney. Serve at once.

Curried eggs: Hard boil 4 eggs, shell and chop, then mix with 2 tablespoons mayonnaise and ½–1 teaspoon curry powder. Serve at once.

Date and cheese: Blend 100 grammes (4 oz) grated Cheddar cheese, 2 tablespoons milk and 50 grammes (2 oz) chopped cooking dates. Serve at once.

Toasted cheese and baked beans: Heat a medium can of baked beans. Spoon on top of the hot buttered toast. Cover each serving of toast and beans with a slice of processed cheese. Put under the grill for about 1 minute, until the cheese starts to melt. Serve at once.

Bengal toasts

This is really an Indian type of recipe, for it mixes curry powder and chutney with the ham, which makes it very tasty. You can use canned ham if you like.

You will need:

bread	4 slices
butter or margarine	40 grammes (1½ oz)
cooked ham	100 grammes (4 oz)
chutney	1 tablespoon
curry powder	½–1 *level* teaspoon

to garnish:
tomatoes   2

These ingredients will make 4 servings.

You will use:

plates for ingredients, basin, sharp knife, chopping board, fork, tablespoon, teaspoon, flat-bladed knife, serving plates.

For success:

Cut the ham into very small pieces so you can mix it with the chutney and other things.

1 Light the gas grill or switch on the electric grill and put the bread on to the top (called the grid) of the grill pan. Do not toast it until you have made the ham mixture.

2 Put half the butter or margarine into a basin.

3 Cut the ham into small pieces on the board, then tip it into the basin.

4 Mash it with the butter or margarine, then add the chutney and curry powder.

5 Toast the bread on both sides, spread with the rest of the butter or margarine, then with the ham mixture.

6 Put back under the grill and heat for 1 minute only.

7 Cut each tomato across the middle.

8 Lift the Bengal toasts on to the warmed serving plates and put a tomato half on top of each serving.

To make a change:

Bengal cheese toasts

1 Follow the recipe for Bengal toasts page 46 up to the end of stage 5.

2 Sprinkle each serving with 1 tablespoon finely grated Cheddar cheese, then continue as stage 6 but allow about 2 minutes under the grill.

3 Continue as stages 7 and 8.

Scrambled eggs

This is delicious for breakfast or supper and there are lots of ways to change the flavour – see pages 50–51.

You will need:

bread	2 slices
butter or margarine	40 grammes (1½ oz)
eggs	3–4
salt	pinch
pepper	shake
milk	2 tablespoons

to garnish:
parsley   sprig

These ingredients will make 2 good servings.

You will use:

plates for ingredients, bread knife and bread board (unless using sliced bread), flat-bladed knife, cup, basin, tablespoon, fork, saucepan, wooden spoon, serving dish or 2 plates.

For success:

Do not cook the eggs too quickly and do not over-cook; remember that they go on cooking in the heat of the saucepan even after the heat is turned off.

1 Light the gas grill or switch on the electric grill.

2 Toast the bread on both sides.

3 Spread with some of the butter or margarine and keep warm. If the serving dish or plates are flame-proof the toast could be placed on these and be put under the grill: if they are oven-proof they can be put into the oven; otherwise keep them in a warm place – over the plate rack or in the warming drawer.

4 Break each egg into the cup, then pour into the basin.

5 Add the salt, pepper and milk and whisk lightly with the fork.

6 Put the rest of the butter or margarine into the saucepan.

7 Light the gas burner or switch on the electric hotplate.

8 Heat the butter or margarine until it has just melted.

9 Add the eggs and start to cook SLOWLY, without stirring.

10 As soon as the eggs begin to set stir GENTLY with the wooden spoon. Do not over-stir.

11 When the eggs are set like a thick cream, take the saucepan away from the cooker and spoon the scrambled eggs on to the hot toast. Serve at once with a tiny piece of parsley on top of each serving.

To make a change:

Cheesey eggs: The ingredients are the same as for scrambled eggs, but add 2–3 tablespoons grated Cheddar cheese at stage 10.

Ham scrambled eggs: Ingredients as for scrambled eggs, but add 2–3 tablespoons chopped cooked ham at stage 10.

Atlantic eggs

1 Ingredients as the scrambled eggs.

2 Open a small can of tuna fish, pink salmon, shrimps or prawns, or use any cooked smoked fish (haddock, cod or kippers) that might have been left over. ALWAYS BE CAREFUL WHEN USING UP LEFT-OVER FISH as stale food can cause food poisoning and fish is particularly likely to do this.

3 Remove any skin and bones from the fish, then flake or chop it; do not use the liquid from canned fish in this recipe.

4 Add the fish at stage 8 of the recipe and heat with the butter or margarine.

5 Add the eggs (see stage 9) and continue as the recipe.

Fish twists

You will need:

fish fingers	8
streaky bacon	4 rashers

These ingredients make 4 large portions.

You will use:

chopping board, kitchen scissors or sharp knife, 8 wooden cocktail sticks, fish slice, serving dish.

For success:

Have the grill hot when you begin.

1 Light the gas grill or switch on the electric grill.

2 Separate the fish fingers. Cut the rinds from the bacon, and cut each rasher lengthways so you have 8 strips.

3 Wind these in a spiral (like the picture) round the fish fingers and put in the cocktail sticks to hold them together.

4 Put them on to the rack (grid) of the grill pan; cook under the hot grill for 2 minutes. Turn over and grill quickly on the other side for 2 minutes.

5 Lower the heat of the grill and finish cooking for 5–6 minutes.

Hot milk drinks

In the first *Piccolo Cook Book* you had recipes for coffee, tea and some milky drinks, but I thought you would like some more ideas. I have included them in this section on snacks and supper dishes because as you know, milk drinks make a nutritious snack in themselves. The following recipes are all made with hot milk and are served in a large mug, cup or tumbler. (Make sure the tumbler is strong enough to hold hot milk.)

Banana whip: Mash a small banana with 1 tablespoon sugar (brown sugar is very good). Divide it between 2 mugs, cups or tumblers. Add hot milk to these.

Honey and cinnamon milk: Put $\frac{1}{2}$–1 tablespoon honey into each mug, cup or tumbler. Add the hot milk and sprinkle ground cinnamon over the top.

Marshmallow surprise: Heat the milk, pour it into the mug, cup or tumbler. Float about 4 marshmallows on top (choose the pink ones if possible, they look prettier). Serve with a spoon, so that you can eat the half-melted marshmallows.

Peppermint milk: Heat the milk and pour it into the mug, cup or tumbler. Float 2–3 plain or chocolate-coated peppermint creams in the milk and stir gently so that they dissolve.

53

Cold milk drinks

These cold milk drinks look nicer in a
glass tumbler than in a cup or mug.

If you make the edge of the tumbler
damp by dipping it in cold water, then
turn it upside down over a plate with a
little castor sugar, you have a very
pretty edge.

Mocha surprise: Put a spoonful of
chocolate ice cream into the tumbler.
Half fill with fairly weak coffee, top with
really cold milk.

Ginger fizz: Half fill the tumbler with
really cold milk, then top with ginger
beer or ginger ale.

Peppermint ice cream soda: Half fill the
tumbler with really cold milk. Add
enough soda water to make the drink
come three-quarters of the way up the
tumbler. Float 2–3 teaspoons ice cream
and 2–3 plain or chocolate-coated
peppermint creams on top. Serve with a
teaspoon.

Banana ice cream soda: Half fill the
tumbler with really cold milk. Add
enough soda water to make the drink
come three-quarters of the way up the
tumbler. Add a tablespoon of strawberry
ice cream and a few banana slices.

Croque Monsieur

This is a very well-known French recipe.
It is very easy and quick to make. You
can use canned ham for the filling.
There is another recipe for fried
sandwiches called Cheese dreams in the
first *Piccolo Cook Book* on page 60.

You will need:

bread	4 large slices
butter or margarine	25 grammes (1 oz)
Gruyère, Cheddar or	
processed cheese	2 slices
cooked ham	2 slices
for coating:	
egg	1
milk	2 tablespoons
for frying:	
fat	50 grammes (2 oz)

*These ingredients will make 4 small or 2
larger servings.*

You will use:
plates for ingredients, sharp knife,
bread board, flat-bladed knife, large
shallow dish, tablespoon, fork, frying
pan, fish slice, serving plate.

For success:

Do not over-cook the sandwiches
otherwise the cheese will be tough.

1 Cut four slices of bread, or take four
slices of ready cut bread.

2 Spread the bread with butter or
margarine.

3 Cover 2 slices of bread with layers of
cheese and ham; top with the other slices
of bread.

4 Cut each sandwich into half.

5 Break the egg on to the shallow dish,
add the milk and beat with the fork.

6 Carry the dish near the cooker so you
do not have egg 'drips' on the floor.

7 Dip the sandwiches into the egg
mixture for ½ minute only, then turn them
over and dip the second side in the egg
mixture.

8 Put the fat into the frying pan.

9 Light the gas burner or switch on the
electric hotplate.

10 Heat the fat until it has just melted –
do not get it too hot; then lower the
heat.

11 Lift the first sandwich off the dish
and put it carefully into the fat. Do
this with the other sandwiches.

12 Cook the sandwiches for nearly $1\frac{1}{2}$
minutes on the bottom side, turn over
with the fish slice and cook for the same
time on the second side.

13 Lift out on to the warmed serving
plate and serve at once.
These are very good with a salad or raw
tomatoes.

To make a change:

Fried ham and chutney sandwiches:
Spread one slice of buttered bread
with chutney, then top with the ham and
the second slice of buttered bread. Do
not use cheese, but dip the sandwiches
into the egg and milk and cook as the
recipe above.

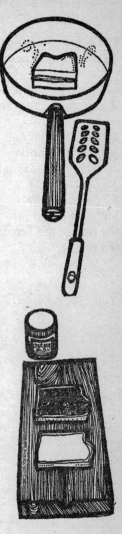

Fried salmon and cottage cheese sandwiches

1 For this you need 6 slices of bread, but no more butter or margarine.

2 Open a can of pink salmon, drain away the liquid and remove any skin and bones.

3 Flake the fish and mix with 2–3 tablespoons cottage cheese (or cream cheese) and seasoning.

4 Spread the fish mixture on 3 slices of buttered bread (see stage 3), cover with the rest of the bread and continue as the recipe.

Beef stuffed tomatoes

This is a good way of using up a small piece of corned beef with some large tomatoes. You can also include some chives, which are a herb that looks like grass. They have a mild oniony flavour, and can be bought dried or fresh.

You will need:

tomatoes	4 *large*
corned beef	about 75 grammes (3 oz)*
soft breadcrumbs	3 tablespoons
chives	4–5 blades
salt	pinch
pepper	shake

for the topping:
soft breadcrumbs	1½ tablespoons
margarine	knob

*Most cans of corned beef weigh about 325 grammes (12 oz); page 63 gives a recipe to use the rest of the beef.

These ingredients will make 4 small or 2 large servings.

You will use:

plates for ingredients, chopping board, sharp knife, teaspoon, basin, fork, kitchen scissors, baking tin plus serving dish or an oven-proof dish.

For success:

Do not over-cook the tomatoes.

1 Set your oven to moderate, 375°F, 190°C or Gas Mark 5.

2 Cut the tomatoes in halves across the centre; scoop out the centre pulp with a teaspoon and put it into the basin.

3 Chop this up with a knife and fork.

4 Cut the corned beef into small pieces, tip into the basin and mash with the tomato pulp.

5 Add the 3 tablespoons breadcrumbs and the chopped chives (if these are fresh cut into tiny pieces with kitchen scissors).

6 Mix well with the fork, add the salt and pepper.

7 Put the tomatoes on to a baking tin or oven-proof dish.

8 Spoon the mixture into the tomato cases.

9 Sprinkle with the breadcrumbs and put a tiny piece of margarine, about the size of a pea, on top of each tomato half.

10 Carry the dish carefully to the oven, so that the tomato halves do not fall over.

11 Bake for 10 minutes just above the centre of a moderate oven if you like very firm tomatoes, or 15 minutes if you like soft ones, then serve at once.

Note: To make a complete meal you could cook peas or heat baked beans on top of the cooker, to serve with the tomato dish.

More ways to stuff tomatoes

If you like them hot:

Ham stuffed tomatoes: Ingredients as the recipe, but use 75 grammes (3 oz) cooked ham instead of corned beef. Chop the ham at stage 4. You could use chopped cooked tongue or beef or lamb or pork or chicken too.

Egg stuffed tomatoes: Ingredients as the recipe, but use 2 large eggs instead of the corned beef. Break the eggs, beat lightly and add to the chopped tomato (stage 4), and continue as the recipe.

If you like them cold:

1 Halve the tomatoes as stage 2, take out the centres and chop, as stage 3.

2 Mix this with *one of the following:*
a 50 grammes (2 oz) diced Cheddar cheese.
b 2–3 chopped hard boiled eggs.
c 75 grammes (3 oz) chopped corned beef or cooked meat.
d 75 grammes (3 oz) well-drained flaked cooked or canned fish of any kind.

3 Add only **2** tablespoons breadcrumbs, the chopped chives, salt and pepper.

4 Put the filling into the tomato cases.

Corned beef hamburgers

You will need:

corned beef	approx 250 grammes (9 oz)*
onion	1 small
potato	1 medium
salt	pinch
pepper	shake

for frying:
fat   50 grammes (2 oz)

to garnish:
parsley or
watercress   small bunch

*Most cans of corned beef weigh about 325 grammes (12 oz); page 59 gives a recipe to use the rest of the beef.

These ingredients will make 4 large or 6 smaller hamburgers.

You will use:

plates for ingredients, sharp knife, chopping board, basin, fork, potato peeler or small vegetable knife, grater, flat knife, frying pan, fish slice, serving dish.

For success:

Press the beef mixture well at stage 6 so that the hamburgers keep a firm shape. Turn carefully at stage 10.

1 Cut the corned beef into small pieces, then tip into the basin and mash with a fork; this is quite easy to do.

2 Peel the onion and the potato, keep the potato in a basin of water or covered with foil until you are ready to grate it, as it turns a black colour very easily. If you have put the potato into water dry it well before grating it.

3 Rub the onion and then the potato against the coarse side of the grater, and allow the grated pieces of vegetable to drop into the basin containing the corned beef.

4 Mix the beef with the grated onion, potato, salt and pepper.

5 Take the mixture out of the basin and divide into 4 or 6 portions.

6 Pat each portion into a neat round cake.

7 Put the fat into a frying pan and put this on to the cooker.

8 Light the gas burner or switch on the electric hotplate.

9 Heat the fat until it has melted. DO NOT HAVE THE HEAT TOO HIGH.

10 Put in the hamburgers and cook for 3 minutes on one side. Turn over one hamburger; if this looks light brown on the one side, you have cooked the meat cakes for sufficiently long on that side, so turn over all the other hamburgers. You will find it is easier to lift them with a fish slice than with a knife.

11 Cook for 3 minutes on the second side, WATCH THE HEAT CAREFULLY AND TURN IT DOWN if you find the hamburgers are cooking too quickly.

12 Lift out of the pan on to a hot dish. Arrange the washed parsley or watercress round the hamburgers.

Note: To make a complete meal cook cauliflower or another green vegetable to serve with the hamburgers.

Beef hamburgers

1 You make these like the corned beef hamburgers on page 63 but use ¼ kilo (½ lb) uncooked minced beef instead of the corned beef.

2 As the meat is not cooked you will need to cook the meat cakes for at least 10 minutes, so lower the heat after browning on either side to make sure the mixture is cooked through to the middle.

3 These can be served with vegetables for a main meal or you can serve them the American way.

4 Split and toast flat round rolls or 'baps', put the hamburger on the bottom half of the roll, then cover with the top half.

5 You can put a little tomato ketchup on the hamburger before adding the top part of the roll.

To make a change:

If you have no rolls serve the hamburgers on pieces of toast and make them look more interesting by garnishing with halved tomatoes.

Cheeseburgers

1 For this recipe you can make your own hamburgers, as described on pages 63 to 66, or you can use ready made frozen hamburgers. You will also need 4 tablespoons grated cheese.

2 Cook the hamburgers as in the recipe or follow the instructions on the packet.

3 When the hamburgers are cooked place them on an oven-proof serving dish, or put them on toasted rolls or slices of toast and then on the serving dish.

4 Set your oven to moderate or moderately hot, 375–400°F, 190–200°C or Gas Mark 5–6.

5 Sprinkle the grated cheese on top of the hamburgers, then put the dish into the oven for 5 minutes only, until the cheese has melted. Serve at once.

To make a change:

Put a ring of well-drained canned pineapple on top of the cooked hamburgers, then top with the cheese at stage 5.

Spread the hamburgers with tomato chutney or tomato ketchup, then top with the cheese at stage 5.

Sardine crisp

This makes sardines into a more interesting snack.

You will need:

bread	4 slices
sardines	1 medium can
Cheddar cheese	50 grammes (2 oz)
breadcrumbs	2 tablespoons
milk	2 tablespoons
salt	pinch
pepper	shake

These ingredients will make 4 servings.

You will use:

plates for ingredients, bread knife and bread board (unless using sliced bread), basin, grater, tablespoon, flat-bladed knife, serving dish or 4 plates.

For success:

Have the grill really hot, so the cheese topping browns quickly.

1 Light the gas grill or switch on the electric grill.

2 Toast the bread on both sides.

3 Open the can of sardines, or ask a grown-up to do this for you.

4 Drain the oil from the can of sardines into the basin, then lift the sardines out and put them on to the hot toast (there is no need to spread the toast with butter or margarine).

5 Grate the cheese and add to the sardine oil in the basin.

6 Mix in the breadcrumbs and milk, then the salt and pepper, stir with the knife.

7 Spread this mixture on top of the sardines and heat for about 3 minutes under the grill.

8 Lift off the grill pan on to the hot dish or plates and serve at once.

To make a change:

You could use this breadcrumb and cheese topping over:
a cooked tomatoes on toast.
b baked beans on toast.
c cooked mushrooms on toast.
As you would not have the oil from the sardines you would need to add 1 tablespoon of salad oil at stage 4.

It would not be as easy to spread the topping over the foods suggested above; you would just sprinkle it on, then brown it at stage 7.

69

Salmon pie

This is a very delicious supper dish.
You can use a packet of instant mashed
potato instead of cooking fresh potatoes.
Pink salmon is cheaper than red salmon,
and very good in this recipe.

You will need:

for the potato topping:

potatoes	½ kilo (1 lb)
salt	¼ level teaspoon
margarine	25 grammes (1 oz)
milk	2 tablespoons
pepper	shake

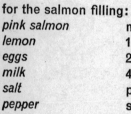

for the salmon filling:

pink salmon	medium can
lemon	1
eggs	2
milk	4 tablespoons
salt	pinch
pepper	shake

to garnish:

parsley	sprig

These ingredients will make 4 servings.

You will use:

plates for ingredients, bowl, potato
peeler or sharp knife, saucepan, sieve or
colander, fork, potato masher, tablespoon,
wooden spoon, can opener, basin, sharp
knife, chopping board, lemon squeezer,
cup, oven-proof serving dish, flat-bladed
knife.

For success:

Cook the potatoes carefully, so you have
a very smooth topping.

1 Fill a bowl with cold water, so you can
put the potatoes into this as you peel
them; this saves them going black.

2 Half fill the saucepan with water, add
the salt, take to the cooker.

3 Light the gas burner or switch on the
electric hotplate.

4 Bring the water to the boil, add the
potatoes, cover the pan and turn down
the heat, for potatoes should cook
steadily.

5 Test to see if the potatoes are soft
after about 20 minutes; use the tip of a
knife. If they are not quite ready let them
go on cooking for a little longer.

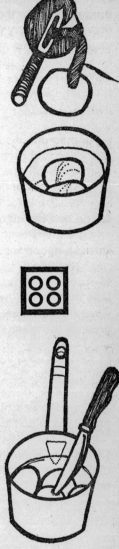

6 When the potatoes are cooked turn off or switch off the heat, then ask a grown-up to carry the pan of very hot vegetables to the sink.

7 Watch how they strain the vegetables through a sieve or colander – also see page 82.

8 Tip the potatoes back into the saucepan and break up with a fork, then continue beating with the fork or with a potato masher until they are quite soft.

9 Add half the margarine, save the rest, and gradually beat in the milk. Use a wooden spoon for this.

10 Add the pepper, then taste and add a little more salt if necessary.
Keep the potatoes in the pan while you prepare the filling.

11 Set your oven to moderate, 375°F, or 190°C or Gas Mark 5.

12 Open the can of salmon, or ask a grown-up to do this for you.

13 Tip the salmon into a basin and take out the skin and the bones as you do not use these.

14 Halve the lemon and squeeze the juice from one half. Cut the other half into 2 or 3 slices, this is quite an awkward job, so you may prefer to ask a grown-up to help. These slices are for garnish.

15 Mix the lemon juice with the salmon.

16 Break the first egg into a cup, then tip it into the salmon; repeat with the second egg.

17 Add the milk, salt and pepper and mix together well with a fork.

18 Spoon the fish mixture into the oven-proof dish.

19 Spoon the potato mixture on top.

20 Smooth this neatly with the knife, then mark with the prongs of a fork.

21 Dot the rest of the margarine over the top in very tiny pieces.

22 Bake in the centre of a moderate oven for 30 minutes.

23 Lift out and put a sprig of parsley and the lemon slices on top.

To make a change:

Tuna pie: Use canned tuna fish instead of salmon.

Fish pie: Simmer ½ kilo (1 lb) white fish or smoked haddock fillet in water until tender, this takes about 10 minutes. Add a little salt when cooking white fish – cod, fresh haddock, etc, but no salt when cooking smoked haddock. Make sure the water does not boil too quickly.

Strain the fish in the same way as vegetables, page 82, put it into a basin and take away any skin.

You then make the recipe in exactly the same way as salmon pie, stages 14–17, page 73.

Bacon and spaghetti hotch potch

This is a splendid dish for supper. It takes only a few minutes to cook and you cook everything in the one big frying pan or saucepan.

You will need:

bacon	4 rashers
margarine	small knob
spaghetti in tomato sauce	1 medium can
eggs	4
milk	4 tablespoons
salt	pinch

These ingredients will make 4 servings.

You will use:

plates for ingredients, kitchen scissors or a sharp knife and chopping board, large frying pan, small knife, can opener, wooden spoon, cup, basin, tablespoon, fork, serving plates.

For success:

Do not over-cook at stage 10 otherwise the mixture will be dry.

1 Cut off the bacon rinds and cut the bacon into neat strips with the kitchen scissors or a sharp knife on the chopping board.

75

2 Put the bacon rinds and the bacon pieces into the frying pan, and place this on the burner or hotplate.

3 Light the gas burner or switch on the electric hotplate.

4 Cook the bacon and the bacon rinds for 2 minutes, then put a piece of margarine from the packet – about the size of a walnut – into the frying pan.

5 Move the frying pan away from the heat and lift out the bacon rinds – you will not eat these, but they have given extra fat.

6 Open the can of spaghetti or ask a grown-up to do this.

7 Tip the spaghetti into the pan and put it back over the heat; stir well with a wooden spoon.

8 Break the first egg into the cup, then tip it into the basin; continue like this with the other eggs.

9 Add the milk and salt; beat with a fork.

10 Pour the egg mixture into the pan, *lower* the heat and stir carefully for 2–3 minutes only, then serve at once.

Speedy pizzas

Pizza pie is a dish you will find when
you visit Italy; this is a very quick version
of that well-known savoury.

You will need:

tomatoes	4 large
water	2 tablespoons
onion	1 small
salt	pinch
pepper	shake
round rolls	4 large
anchovy fillets	1 can
Cheddar cheese	about 50 grammes (2 oz)

Little butter or margarine (optional)

These ingredients will make 4 large or 8 small servings.

You will use:

plates for ingredients, chopping board,
sharp knife, saucepan, tablespoon,
grater, wooden spoon, flat knife, fish
slice, serving dish.

For success:

Have the grill very hot before heating
the pizzas at stage 10.

1 Cut the tomatoes into slices, then put
into a saucepan with the water.

77

2 Peel the onion and rub against the coarse side of the grater; let the onion drop into the saucepan.

3 Light the gas burner or switch on the electric hotplate.

4 Cook the tomato mixture for about 5 minutes until it becomes quite thick. Stir with the wooden spoon as the mixture cooks, so that it does not burn.

5 Take the pan off the heat and add the salt and pepper to the tomato mixture.

6 Split the rolls and toast them under the grill; you can spread them with butter or margarine if you like.

7 Spread the tomato mixture over the halved rolls and stand them in the grill pan.

8 Open the can of anchovy fillets or ask a grown-up to do this for you. Lift out the anchovy fillets and arrange them on top of the tomato mixture in a neat design.

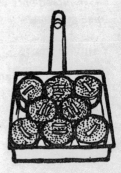

9 Grate the cheese and sprinkle it over the top of the tomato and anchovy mixture.

10 Put under the hot grill and heat for about 2 minutes, until the cheese has melted, then lift on to a serving dish and serve at once.

Note: You could cook the tomato mixture earlier in the day, so it is quite ready before you make the pizzas.

To make a change:
Use canned sardines in place of anchovy fillets.

Use cooked ham and cut this into neat strips and use instead of anchovy fillets.

Cheese and apple salad

This is a very pretty salad for a party supper dish.

You will need:

lettuce	1
mayonnaise or	
salad dressing	4 tablespoons
milk	1 tablespoon
vinegar	1 teaspoon
red-skinned dessert	
apples	2
orange	1
Cheddar cheese	about 200 grammes (8 oz)

These ingredients will make 4–5 servings.

You will use:

plates for ingredients, salad shaker or cloth, tablespoon, teaspoon, mixing bowl, chopping board, sharp knife, serving dish.

For success:

Put the apple into the mayonnaise mixture as soon as it is cut. This stops it turning a brown colour.

1 Wash the lettuce in cold water. Shake dry in a salad shaker or pat *gently* in a cloth.

2 Put the mayonnaise, milk and vinegar into the mixing bowl.

3 Wash and dry, but do not peel, the apples. Put them on to the chopping board; halve, then quarter, and cut away the cores.

4 Cut the apples into neat small pieces, or ask a grown-up to do this for you.

5 Tip into the mayonnaise mixture and stir.

6 Peel the orange. Put the segments of fruit on to the chopping board or on to a plate and cut neatly, then add to the apple mixture.

7 Put the cheese on to the chopping board cut it into neat pieces and add it to the apple mixture.

8 Lay the lettuce on the serving dish and spoon the cheese and apple mixture in the centre.

Did you know?

There are several ways to chop parsley. Always wash AND dry the parsley first and remove all the stalks.

1 Put the sprigs on to a chopping board and chop in a clockwise direction. As you will see from the picture the finger tips of your left hand support one end of the knife (the non-cutting edge).

81

2 Use kitchen scissors. This is a good way as the parsley juice is not wasted.

3 Use one of the special choppers.

Did you know?

The way to tell if fat is hot enough for frying is to melt the fat and put a tiny cube of bread into the pan; if it turns golden brown *in about 1 minute* you can cook the food. If it burns or browns more quickly allow the fat to cool slightly and test again.

Always pull the frying pan away from the heat as you test.

Did you know?

There are two ways of straining vegetables. Both mean handling hot saucepans filled with hot food and liquid, so a grown-up should do them generally.

1 Take the pan to the sink and tilt the lid so the liquid can run into the sink, or into a large basin in the sink. This is very difficult.

2 Put a colander or big sieve over a large basin in the sink or put these into the sink. Tip the vegetables *carefully* into the sieve or colander. MIND THE STEAM.

MAKE A GOOD DINNER

If you can cook a complete dinner it will be a lovely surprise and treat for the family, and I am sure you can do it well if you plan everything carefully.

Never try to cook a whole dinner yourself without asking permission from your parents, for food (particularly meat or chicken) is expensive and they may prefer to help you.

If they say 'yes' then you can feel very proud of doing such an important job.

Meal in a parcel

This meal 'looks after itself' as you wrap all the food in squares of aluminium foil.

You will need:

lamb chops	4 lean
tomatoes	4 large
potatoes	4 large
salt	pinch
pepper	shake
frozen peas	1 packet
margarine	15 grammes ($\frac{1}{2}$ oz)

These ingredients will make 4 servings.

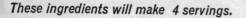

You will use:

plates for ingredients, aluminium foil,
kitchen scissors, sharp knife, chopping
board, potato peeler or vegetable knife,
bowl, baking or meat tin, serving dish.

For success:

Wrap the foil parcels lightly.

1 Look at the lamb chops and if they
seem to have a lot of fat cut this away,
then decide on the size of the aluminium
squares – you need 4 for the chops,
tomatoes and potatoes and 1 large one for
the peas.

2 Put the 4 lamb chops in the middle of
4 good sized squares of foil.

3 Cut each tomato in 3–4 thick slices and
put these on top of the chops.

4 Peel the potatoes and cut into 6–7
thin slices, or ask a grown-up to do this
for you; keep the potatoes in a bowl of
water as you peel them so they do not
discolour.

5 Put the potato slices over the tomatoes
and add the salt and pepper. Wrap up
these four parcels carefully.

6 Put the block of frozen peas on the large piece of foil, add the margarine, salt and pepper, and wrap up carefully.

7 Place the 5 foil parcels on to the baking or meat tin.

8 You can set the oven before you begin this recipe, but this is the kind of meal you can put into an automatic oven and leave for some time; ask a grown-up to tell you about this kind of oven. Set your oven to moderate, 375°F, 190°C or Gas Mark 5.

9 Put the parcels into the centre of the moderate oven.

10 Leave for 55 minutes, then lift out carefully.

11 Ask a grown-up to open the parcels for you or use oven gloves, for a lot of steam comes out.

12 Lift the food on to a hot dish.

13 You may need to strain the peas, see page 82. Serve at once.

A roast dinner

A roast meal, such as you might eat for
a Sunday lunch, sounds complicated but
in fact it is not difficult to cook. It does
mean taking great care not to hurt
yourself on hot tins, and it does mean
'dishing up' in the right order, so that
none of the food becomes cold before
it is served.
Page 94 tells you about this.

As meat for roasting is expensive, you
will probably need a grown-up's
agreement before tackling the following
menu:

Roast lamb
Mint sauce
Roast potatoes
Cauliflower or other green vegetable
Fruit trifle (see page 144)
or fruit salad and cream (see page 145)

You will need:

ingredients for fruit trifle (page 144) or
fruit salad (page 145)

potatoes	about ¾ kilo (1½lb)
lamb	½ leg or ½ shoulder
fat	50 grammes (2 oz)

for the sauce:

mint	small bunch
sugar	1–2 tablespoons
vinegar	2 tablespoons

cauliflower	1
salt	very good pinch

for the gravy:

flour	1 tablespoon
gravy browning	½ tablespoon
*water**	⅛ litre (142 ml) or ¼ pint
*vegetable water**	⅛ litre (142 ml) or ¼ pint
fat from cooking the meat	1 tablespoon

*You may prefer to use stock made by
simmering meat bones in water.

*These ingredients will make 4 servings.
There will probably be some cooked meat
left. This can be served cold.*

You will use:

plates for ingredients, utensils for
trifle or fruit salad, pages 144 or 145,
potato peeler or vegetable knife, bowl,
roasting tin, kitchen paper, sharp knife,
chopping board (or kitchen scissors), 2
sauce boats, 2 tablespoons, clean
teacloth (or use kitchen paper), meat dish,
serving dish for cauliflower, serving
plates, colander, 1 fairly large saucepan
with lid, 1 smaller saucepan, teaspoon,
wooden spoon, basin, fish slice.

For success:

Make out your timetable and work
carefully and steadily through this; do
not try and do too many things at one
time.

1 Make the trifle or fruit salad before
you prepare the meat and potatoes, so
that it is quite ready. You could make the
trifle the day beforehand, but the fruit
salad is nicer if prepared only a few
hours before it is served.

2 Put the trifle or fruit salad into a cool
place.

3 Peel the potatoes and keep in a bowl of
cold water so they do not become dark
in colour – *halve large potatoes.*

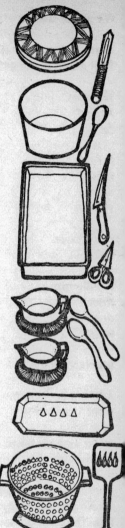

4 Weigh the meat, or look at the ticket from the butcher or supermarket; this is important, for you work out the cooking time according to the weight of the meat. When cooking lamb you allow 20 minutes for each ½ kilo (1 lb) plus an extra 20 minutes.

A joint weighing 1½ kilo (3 lb) would take

3 × 20 minutes	= 1 hour
plus extra 20 minutes	= 20 minutes

Total cooking time = 1 hour 20 minutes

5 Put the meat into the roasting tin, and it is a good idea to choose a tin sufficiently large to cook the potatoes in it as well as the meat.

6 Add the fat to the meat in the tin; if you are roasting lamb without roasting potatoes you will not need this fat.

7 Now look at the clock. You do not want to heat the oven, or put the meat into the oven too soon for if you do it will be over-cooked.

8 If you are putting the meat into *a cold oven*, then lighting the gas or switching on the electric oven, add an extra 10 minutes to your total cooking time; the meat starts to cook in the heating-up period.

If you are putting the meat into *a heated oven*, then light the gas or switch on the electric oven and wait 15 minutes before putting in the meat.

9 Let us imagine you want the meat at 1 PM and that the joint takes 1 hour 20 minutes to cook and that you are putting the meat into a cold oven. This is the timetable to follow:

10 *11·25 AM :* put the meat in its tin (with the fat) into the oven.

In most gas ovens you put it towards the top of the oven.

In many electric ovens too you can put it near the top of the oven, but in some other electric cookers it is better to put the meat in its tin at the bottom of the oven – *check with your mother or with the card or book that goes with your cooker.*

11 Set your oven to moderately hot: usually 400°F, 200°C or Gas Mark 5–6. Cookers vary slightly so *just check* with the card or book that goes with your cooker.

12 You can now prepare the mint sauce. Wash the mint in cold water and take the leaves from the stalks. Pat these dry on kitchen paper. Chop the mint with a sharp knife (this is quite difficult) on the chopping board, or use kitchen scissors. Pages 81–82 tell you how to chop parsley, and mint is chopped in the same way.

13 Put the mint into the sauce boat, add the sugar and vinegar, and stir well. *Note:* if you don't know anyone who grows mint, you can sometimes find it in supermarkets or greengrocers. Otherwise, buy a jar of mint concentrate and follow the directions on it.

14 *11·50 AM:* lift the potatoes out of the bowl of cold water and dry them very well on kitchen paper or a clean teacloth.

15 *11·55 AM:* AT THIS STAGE YOU MUST BE VERY CAREFUL, OR YOU MUST ASK A GROWN-UP TO HELP YOU.
Open the oven door and take the meat tin out of the oven. You must have STRONG OVEN GLOVES and you must make sure NO ONE IS NEAR ENOUGH TO DISTRACT YOU or is playing in the kitchen. Put the very hot tin down – MAKE SURE YOU DO NOT BURN ANY SURFACE – some modern laminated working surfaces can

be harmed with very hot tins, so it is a good idea to put a cork mat under the tin. MAKE SURE THE TIN CANNOT BE TIPPED OVER. Close the oven door.

16 Put the potatoes into the hot fat.

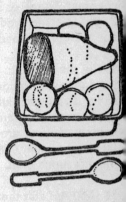

17 Now take the 2 tablespoons and turn the potatoes round in the hot fat, so that they look greasy on all sides.

18 Open the oven door again and put the tin back into the oven.

19 There is no need to touch the tin or oven again until it is time to dish up.

20 *12·5 PM:* prepare the cauliflower. You can cook it whole, but you save more of the Vitamin C (see page 27) if you divide the flower part into neat sprigs. Use some of the inner green stalks, but not the very outside stalks. Wash the cauliflower in cold water, then lift it into a colander and allow it to drain.

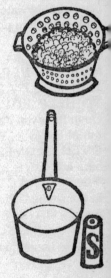

21 *12·15 PM:* put the serving dishes and the plates to warm.

22 *12·20 PM:* Fill the larger saucepan with water to a height of about 8 cm (3 inches) and add a very good pinch of salt (or use $\frac{1}{4}$ teaspoon).

23 Take this to the cooker, and light the gas burner or switch on the electric hotplate.

24 *12·25 PM:* blend the flour and gravy browning with ⅛ litre (¼ pint) of water in a basin.

25 Tip into the smaller saucepan.

26 *12·30 PM:* carry the cauliflower in the colander to the cooker. If you stand the colander on a plate you will have no 'drips' of cold water.

27 Put the cauliflower into the boiling water and cover the saucepan with a lid.

28 *12·45 PM:* turn off the burner or hotplate. Take the cauliflower pan to the sink and strain this or ask a grown-up to do this (see page 82). Save ⅛ litre (142 ml) or ¼ pint of the liquid. Put the cauliflower into a serving dish *and keep it warm.*

29 Pour the ⅛ litre (¼ pint) cauliflower water into the flour and gravy browning saucepan (see stages 24 and 25).

30 Light the gas burner or switch on the electric hotplate again and stir the gravy with the wooden spoon until it thickens; turn the heat very low to keep it hot.

31 *12·58 PM:* take the meat tin out of the oven. REMEMBER ALL THE POINTS MENTIONED IN STAGE 15.

32 Lift the meat and potatoes on to the hot meat dish – a fish slice is good for this.

33 Turn off the burner or hotplate and carry the gravy saucepan VERY CAREFULLY over to the meat tin. Stir in 1 tablespoon of the fat from the tin. If the gravy is really hot you will not need to cook it again.

34 Pour the gravy into the sauce boat and the meal is ready.

As you will see you have to be rather quick between stages 26 to 34.

You may find it easier to dish up the meat and potatoes a little earlier and keep them hot, in which case start the cooking 5 minutes earlier.

Grown-ups will probably prefer to dish up the cauliflower at the last minute – this is the best way to cook vegetables, so they are not being kept warm for too long – but you will need practice to do everything 'all at once' and it is better to work steadily when you are learning to cook.

Hunter's chicken casserole

This is a very good way of cooking chicken; you do not need to make a gravy and the tomatoes and vegetables in the recipe take the place of a green vegetable. Serve with jacket potatoes to make a good meal.

You will need:

frying chicken	4 portions
potatoes	4 medium
margarine	50 grammes (2 oz)
tomatoes	1 medium can
onion	1 large
carrot	1 large
salt	good pinch
pepper	good shake

to garnish:	
parsley	small sprig

These ingredients will make 4 servings.

You will use:

plates for ingredients, kitchen paper, scrubbing brush, baking tray, fork, flat-bladed knife, oven-proof casserole with a lid, 2 tablespoons, can opener, basin, sharp knife, grater, teacloth, vegetable dish for potatoes.

For success:

Let the chicken brown at stage 10 before you add the tomato mixture.
Do not over-cook chicken; it makes it very dry.

1 If you are using portions of frozen chicken allow these to thaw (defrost) at room temperature before cooking. This must be done thoroughly and will take 8–12 hours. If using joints of fresh chicken wash them in cold water, then dry them on kitchen paper. Dry frozen chicken in the same way when it has defrosted.

2 Set your oven to very moderate, 325–350°F, 170–180°C or Gas Mark 3–4.

3 Scrub and dry the potatoes, put them on the baking tray (this makes it easier to take them out of the oven), and prick them with a fork so that they do not burst their skins.

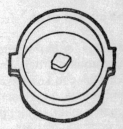

4 Put the potatoes towards the top of the oven.

5 Put the margarine into the casserole, place it in the centre of the oven and leave it for 5 minutes so that the margarine melts.

6 Remove the casserole from the oven; read pages 91–92, stage 15, about taking hot tins or dishes from a hot oven.

7 Put the casserole on to the working surface, taking care it does not harm this; it is always a good idea to put a pan stand or cork mat under hot dishes.

8 Add the pieces of chicken and turn them in the melted margarine with the 2 tablespoons.

9 Put the casserole back into the oven; do not cover it for you want the chicken to brown slightly.

10 Leave the chicken for 15 minutes without touching it.

11 Meanwhile, open the can of tomatoes, or ask a grown-up to do this for you.

12 Tip the tomatoes into a basin, and chop them with a knife and fork.

13 Grate the peeled onion and carrot into the tomatoes. Add the salt and pepper.

14 Take the casserole with the chicken out of the oven – do this very carefully.

15 Put the casserole on to the working surface. Be careful to stand it on a mat, so that it does not harm the working surface.

16 Allow the casserole to stand for about 5 minutes, then pour the tomato mixture over the chicken. If you pour the cold tomato mixture over the very hot chicken you could crack an oven-proof glass dish.

17 Put the lid on the casserole, replace it in the centre of the oven and leave for 40 minutes.

18 Remove the casserole from the oven.

19 Most casseroles can be used for serving dishes, so take off the lid – DO THIS VERY CAREFULLY FOR THERE WILL BE A LOT OF STEAM COMING FROM THE DISH – and top with parsley.

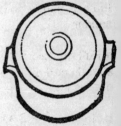

20 Remove the baking tray of potatoes from the oven – BE CAREFUL. Lift each potato from the tray with a folded teacloth and put it into the vegetable dish.

21 The meal is now ready.

Did you know?

There are two ways to separate egg whites from yolks:

1 Have a saucer ready.

a Crack the egg gently on the edge of a cup or saucer, then pull the halves of the egg apart carefully and allow the egg to drop on to the saucer.

b Put an egg cup over the yolk; holding it firmly, pour the egg white into a basin, then take the egg cup away.

2 Have two basins or cups ready. Crack the egg gently on the edge of a cup or saucer.

a Pull the two halves of the shell apart slightly and allow the white to drop into one basin.

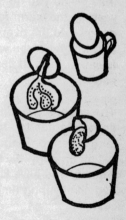

b Now open the egg and pour the yolk into the second basin.

If you have let a little egg yolk drop into the white it will not whip properly, so you must take it out. Use the damp corner of a piece of kitchen paper or the corner of a damp, clean teacloth, or use one half of the egg shell – all these are better than using a teaspoon.

YEAST COOKERY

Yeast cookery is fun because yeast is a living substance that makes your flour mixture rise and grow.

Yeast cookery is not difficult, but here are some things to remember:

If you use fresh yeast make sure it is quite fresh. It should be fairly soft and crumble easily. Keep the yeast well wrapped and store it in the refrigerator until you are ready to use it. If you cannot buy fresh yeast (health food stores generally stock it), buy dried yeast. The recipes tell you about using both fresh and dried yeast.

You will see that the yeast mixture is left to 'prove' – which is another word for 'rise' – and you do this by leaving the yeast in the warm room. Do not put the dough into the oven or anywhere too hot; if you do you will spoil the mixture because you will destroy the yeast too soon.

The recipes tell you to 'knead' the dough; do not do this too roughly or for too long a period. Stage 13 of the bread recipe on page 104 shows how to tell whether you have kneaded for a sufficiently long time.

Home-made bread

A home-made loaf of bread is delicious
and a great treat for the whole family. As
you will see the recipe states 'strong'
flour as this is particularly good for
yeast cookery. You can buy it at good
grocers and health food shops, but if
you cannot find any use ordinary plain
flour. You will not need self-raising flour
or baking powder as the yeast makes
the mixture rise.

You will need:

fresh yeast	15 grammes (½ oz) –
or	do not use any more
dried yeast	2 LEVEL teaspoons
sugar	1 teaspoon
water	generous ¼ litre
	(284 ml) or ½ pint
strong white flour	poor ½ kilo (1 lb)
salt	1 LEVEL teaspoon
milk	about 1 tablespoon

These ingredients will make 1 loaf.

You will use:

plates for ingredients, basin, teaspoon,
flat-bladed knife, saucepan or kettle,
measuring jug, wooden spoon, sieve,
mixing bowl, pastry board, flour dredger,
piece of polythene or clean teacloth,
1 kilo (2 lb) loaf tin, pastry brush, wire
cooling tray.

For success:

Read page 100 again; follow all directions carefully. Do not try and hurry the process of making bread, just leave the dough to rise while you do other jobs.

1 IF USING FRESH YEAST put the yeast into the basin.

2 Add the sugar and mix with a teaspoon until the yeast becomes quite liquid.

3 Light the gas burner or switch on the electric hotplate or kettle.

4 Heat some water in a saucepan or kettle until it is just at blood heat – this means it will feel slightly warm. Do not make it too hot. Pour enough into the measuring jug to give a *good* ¼ litre (284 ml) or ½ pint.

5 Pour MOST of the water over the yeast and sugar, saving just a little of the water. Stir with the wooden spoon.

6 IF USING DRIED YEAST, heat the water as in stage 4 and pour ¼ litre (½ pint) into the measuring jug; then pour most of the water into the basin.

7 Add the sugar, stir well, then sprinkle the dried yeast on top of the water; wait 10 minutes, then stir again.

8 IF USING EITHER FRESH OR DRIED YEAST, sprinkle a very little flour over the top of the yeast mixture and leave for about 15 minutes or until you see the surface is covered with little bubbles.

9 Sieve the flour and salt into the mixing bowl, then make a hollow in the centre of the flour.

10 Pour the yeast mixture into this and mix everything together with the wooden spoon; then put this down and use your hands or a flat-bladed knife.

11 Go on gathering the dough together to make a soft ball. You will probably find you need to add the rest of the water – remember you did not use quite all the ¼ litre (284 ml) or ½ pint water – but it is a good idea not to make the yeast dough too wet to begin with, for different makes of flour vary in the amount of water they need. If the dough is too wet use a generous amount of flour on the pastry board when kneading the dough.

12 Put the ball of dough on to the pastry board or working surface.

13 Shake over a little flour, from the flour dredger, then knead with your hands until smooth.

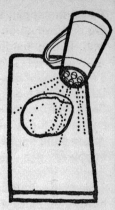

KNEADING yeast dough is done by pulling the dough gently, then folding it back again – pulling, folding all the time. You can tell when the dough has not been kneaded enough by using the following test: Dip your finger in a little flour, then press it into the dough; you will make a mark which does not come out. When you have kneaded enough the mark comes out slowly.

14 Put the kneaded dough back into the bowl and cover with a piece of polythene or a clean teacloth.

15 Leave in a warm room (not in a draught) or in the airing cupboard for about 1 hour, until it has risen to twice the size it was at stage 14 – do not let dough rise more than this.

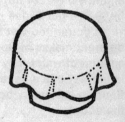

16 Lift the dough from the bowl on to the pastry board again, add a shake of flour and knead once more as described in stage 13.

17 If you are making your loaf in a tin, press out the dough to a neat oblong. A–B should be the length of the loaf tin and A–C and B–D should be about three times the width of the loaf tin. *Note:* if you wish to make a different shaped loaf, see page 109.

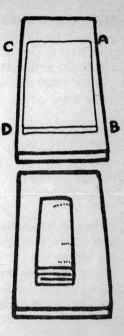

18 Fold the dough in three so you have a shape the same size as the tin. While you are doing this put the loaf tin in a warm place.

19 Grease the tin with oil or melted fat: see page 155 for ways of doing this.

20 Put the folded dough into the tin; press down GENTLY.

21 Set your oven at hot to very hot, 450–475°F, 230–240°C or Gas Mark 7–8.

22 Brush the top of the dough with the milk, then cover the top of the tin very lightly with a piece of polythene or a cloth.

23 Leave the tin in a warm place for about 15–20 minutes to allow the yeast dough to rise again up the tin. You can remove the polythene or cloth towards the end of this period so that it does not touch the dough.

24 Put the tin in the centre of the oven and bake for 15 minutes, then lower the oven heat to very moderate, 325–350°F, 170–180°C or Gas Mark 3–4 and leave for another 15–20 minutes until the bread looks brown.

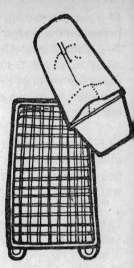

25 Lift the tin out of the oven CAREFULLY and tip the loaf on to a wire cooling tray. This means handling the hot tin and loaf, so you may prefer to ask a grown-up to do this for you.

26 Test to see if the bread is cooked. The way to do this is to tap the bread on the bottom – it should give a 'hollow' sound; if it does not do so, put the bread back into the tin and cook it in the oven for a few more minutes.

Milk bread

This is made in exactly the same way as the bread on page 101, but instead of using water use milk.
The milk must be warmed in exactly the same way as the water (see stages 4, 5 and 6 on page 102).

Fruit bread

This is made in exactly the same way as the bread on page 101, but add 100 grammes (4 oz) sultanas or seedless raisins or currants or mixed dried fruit to the flour and salt at stage 9, page 103.

Wholemeal bread

This is made in exactly the same way as the bread on page 101, but instead of using white flour use all wholemeal (stone-ground) flour.
Wholemeal flour needs more liquid than white flour, so add a little extra warm water at stage 11, page 103, in order to make the dough bind together easily.
When you cook the wholemeal bread turn the heat to very moderate after only 10 minutes in the hot to very hot oven (see stage 24, page 106).

Brown bread

This is made in exactly the same way as the bread on page 101, but instead of using all white flour use half white flour and half wholemeal (stone-ground) flour. You may find you need a little more than a generous $\frac{1}{4}$ litre (284 ml) or $\frac{1}{2}$ pint water to make the dough bind together, at stage 11, page 103. Also, the bread may need a few minutes longer baking in the oven.

Different shapes for bread

There are many shapes for bread and you will enjoy making these.
Here is one you can try.

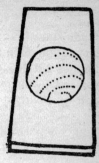

Cottage loaf

1 Follow the recipe for bread from page 101 to stage 16 on page 104.

2 Make two-thirds of the dough into a round at stage 16.

3 Put this on to a greased warm flat baking tray and flatten it a little on top.

4 Make the rest of the dough into a smaller round and put this on top of the bigger round.

5 Press your floured finger in the middle of the top round.

6 Brush the bread with milk and leave to 'prove' (rise) in a warm place for 15–20 minutes.

7 Bake as the tin loaf (stages 24–26, page 106).

Rolls

1 If you know how to make the basic yeast dough as in the home-made bread on pages 101–106, you can also make small rolls, which would be splendid for a picnic or a party.

2 You can make white or milk or brown or wholemeal rolls.

3 Follow the recipe for the home-made bread right up to stage 16 on page 104.

4 Put the dough on to the pastry board and cut it into 16–20 small pieces. Now form each piece into the shape you want. The pictures below show some of the shapes you can make.

Small rounds

Small cottage loaves

Crescent shapes – these are sometimes called horse-shoe rolls.

Straight rolls (called batons) – mark these on top with a a knife to make them look interesting.

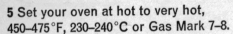

5 Set your oven at hot to very hot, 450–475°F, 230–240°C or Gas Mark 7–8.

6 Lift the shapes on to 2 warmed greased baking trays. Remember that they will rise and spread out as they 'prove', so do not put too many on the same tray and do not put them too close to one another. You can brush the rolls with milk if you wish, but if you like them to be very crisp I would not do this.

7 Allow the rolls to 'prove' in a warm place for 10–15 minutes, until they are nearly twice the size they were at stage 6.

8 Bake the rolls just above the centre of the oven for approximately 12 minutes, until they are golden brown in colour. You will probably find the rolls on the baking tray nearer the top of the oven cook a little before the ones on the lower tray.

9 Take the trays out of the oven CAREFULLY and lift the rolls on to a wire cooling tray.

Note: Bread keeps well for several days, but rolls are nicer if they are eaten the day they are baked, or if you warm them for a few minutes if they have become a little stale.

Hot cross buns

These home-made buns will be appreciated by your family on Good Friday. Make them the day before and just warm them in the oven, to serve for breakfast.

As this recipe uses more sugar, fruit and some fat you use 15 grammes (½ oz) yeast to only 340 grammes (12 oz) flour, whereas with bread 15 grammes (½ oz) will raise ½ kilo (1 lb) flour.

You will need:

fresh yeast	15 grammes (½ oz) –
or	be generous with this
dried yeast	2 LEVEL teaspoons
sugar	50 grammes (2 oz)
water	4 tablespoons
milk	⅛ litre (142 ml) or ¼ pint
strong white flour	340* grammes (12 oz)
salt	pinch
mixed spice	½ teaspoon
ground cinnamon	½–1 teaspoon
margarine	50 grammes (2 oz)
mixed dried fruit (raisins, sultanas, currants)	75–100 grammes (3–4 oz)

to glaze:

sugar	50 grammes (2 oz)
water	2 tablespoons

*This gives a better result than 300 grammes.

These ingredients will make 12–16 buns.

You will use:

plates for ingredients, basin, teaspoon,
measuring jug, saucepan, wooden spoon,
sieve, mixing bowl, flat-bladed knife,
pastry board, flour dredger, piece of
polythene or clean teacloth, 2 baking
trays, sharp knife, small basin or cup,
pastry brush, wire cooling tray.

For success:

Follow the advice on yeast cookery given
on pages 100–111.

1 IF USING FRESH YEAST, put the
yeast into the basin.

2 Add 1 teaspoon of the sugar and mix
with the yeast until it becomes creamy.

3 Light the gas burner or switch on the
electric hotplate.

4 Heat the water and milk together in a
saucepan until they just reach blood
heat. This means the liquid will feel
slightly warm – do not make it too hot.

5 Pour the milk and water over the yeast
and sugar, and stir with a wooden spoon.

113

6 IF USING DRIED YEAST, heat
the water and milk as in stage 4 and pour
it into the basin.

7 Add a teaspoon of the sugar, stir well,
then sprinkle the dried yeast on top of the
liquid, wait for 10 minutes, then stir
again.

8 IF USING FRESH OR DRIED
YEAST, sprinkle a little flour over the
top of the yeast mixture and leave for
about 15 minutes, or until you see the
surface is covered with little bubbles.

9 Sieve the flour, salt, mixed spice and
ground cinnamon into the mixing bowl.

10 Add the margarine to the bowl, and
rub this into the flour mixture until it
looks like fine breadcrumbs.

11 Add the rest of the sugar and the
mixed dried fruit, then make a well in
the centre of the flour mixture and pour
the yeast mixture into this.

12 Mix everything together with the
wooden spoon, then put this down and
use a flat-bladed knife or your hands.

13 Gather the dough together to make a
smooth soft ball. The amount of liquid
should be enough, but if the dough

seems very dry add a VERY little more warm milk or water. If the dough seems a little sticky, use a generous amount of flour in kneading the dough.

14 Knead the dough until smooth. Stage 13 on page 104 tells you how to test when the dough is properly kneaded.

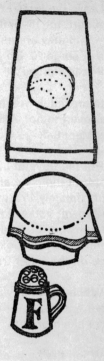

15 When the dough has been kneaded enough put it back into the mixing bowl, cover it with a piece of polythene or a clean teacloth and leave in a warm place for about 1¼–1½ hours, until it has risen to twice the size it was – do not let the dough rise more than this. Bun dough takes longer to rise than bread dough, for the mixture is heavier.

16 Lift the dough from the bowl on to the pastry board again, add a shake of flour and knead again until smooth.

17 Put 2 flat baking trays in a warm place, grease them lightly, see page 155.

18 Cut the dough into about 12–16 pieces.

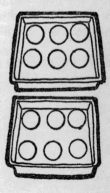

19 Roll each piece into a neat ball and put these on to the trays.

20 Flatten the buns slightly and mark an X (cross) in the centre of each with a knife.

21 Leave the buns in the room or airing cupboard for 15 minutes to 'prove', i.e. rise until they are nearly twice their size at stage 20. Do not cover the buns while they 'prove'.

22 Immediately you have done this set your oven to hot, 425–450°F, 220–230°C or Gas Mark 6–7.

23 Put the trays of buns just above the centre of the oven and bake for approximately 15 minutes until the buns are brown; you will probably find that the buns on the baking tray nearer the top of the oven cook a little before the ones on the lower tray.

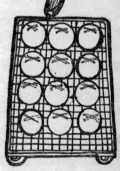

24 While the buns are cooking put the sugar and water for the glaze into a small basin or cup.

25 When the buns are ready remove from the oven and dip the pastry brush into the glaze and brush the buns with this, to give them a shine.

26 Lift the buns off the baking trays on to the wire cooling tray to cool.

Fruit buns

Follow the directions for making hot
cross buns on page 112, and use the same
ingredients but *leave out* the mixed
spice and ground cinnamon and do
not mark the X (cross) on the buns.

Bath buns

1 Use the same ingredients as for hot
cross buns, but leave out the water and
the mixed spice and ground cinnamon.

2 Mix the buns to stage 11, then add 2
eggs (these take the place of the water).

3 Continue the recipe to stage 20.

4 Put the balls on to the warmed greased
baking trays and flatten slightly.

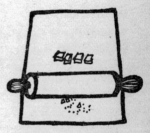

5 Take 6–8 lumps of sugar and put these
on to a piece of greaseproof paper.

6 Crush the lumps of sugar very lightly
with a rolling pin, so you have small
pieces of sugar.

7 Brush the top of the buns with a little
milk. Sprinkle over the pieces of sugar.

8 Continue as in stages 21 to 23, page 116.
Do not use the sugar and water glaze.

9 Lift the buns off the baking trays on
to a wire cooling tray to cool.

INTERESTING PUDDINGS AND DESSERTS

Orange upside down cake

Although this is called a cake, it makes a delicious pudding and on page 121 is the recipe for a sauce to serve with it. You can serve this dish for tea or for a party dish without the sauce. Use jellied marmalade if possible, rather than the thick-cut type.

You will need:

for the glaze:

margarine	25 grammes (1 oz)
jelly marmalade	3 tablespoons
mandarin oranges	1 medium can

for the cake:

margarine	100 grammes (4 oz)
castor sugar	100 grammes (4 oz)
eggs	2
self-raising flour (or plain flour and 1½ level teaspoons baking powder)	150 grammes (6 oz)
milk	1 tablespoon

These ingredients will make 6–8 slices.

You will use:

plates for ingredients, flat-bladed knife, 18 cm (7 inch) cake tin (*without a loose base*) or round or square oven-proof dish, tablespoon, can opener, jug, mixing bowl, wooden spoon, cup, sieve, large serving plate.

For success:

Follow the directions for creaming on page 153 and test the cake carefully at stage 14. Page 154 tells you about testing cakes.

1 Set your oven to very moderate, 325–350°F, or 170–180°C or Gas Mark 3–4.

2 Spread most of the margarine at the bottom of the cake tin or oven-proof dish, and a little round the sides of the tin or dish.

3 Put the marmalade at the bottom of the tin, and spread it out evenly.

4 Make 2 holes in the can of mandarin oranges. This is not easy to do, so it would be a good idea to ask a grown-up to help you.

5 Pour the liquid from the can into the jug, then open the can properly.

6 Tip the orange segments into the tin or dish and spread evenly over the marmalade.

7 Put the margarine and sugar into the mixing bowl.

8 Cream with the wooden spoon until soft and light, see page 153.

9 Break the first egg into a cup, then add to the margarine and sugar, and beat well.

10 Break the second egg into a cup, then add to the margarine and sugar, and beat well.

11 Sieve the self-raising flour (or plain flour and baking powder) into the mixing bowl, then blend into the margarine mixture with an ordinary tablespoon.

12 Lastly, add the milk and mix gently but thoroughly.

See the note on page 153 about how you can cream margarine and sugar very quickly if using the modern soft margarines.

13 Spoon the cake mixture on top of the oranges, scrape the bowl clean, and smooth the mixture very flat on top.

14 Bake for 1¼ hours in the middle of a very moderate oven until firm to the touch; page 154 tells you about testing cakes.

15 Take out of the oven CAREFULLY and let it stand for 3 minutes.

16 Have the large serving plate ready and tip the cake upside down on to this.

17 Serve hot or cold, either by itself or with the orange sauce or with ice cream.

Orange sauce

The sauce is not only very good with the orange upside down cake, but with ice cream. You can serve it hot or cold.

You will need:

syrup	from the canned mandarin oranges
orange marmalade	2 tablespoons
orange	1
cornflour	2 LEVEL teaspoons

These ingredients will make 6–8 servings.

You will use:

jug, saucepan, tablespoon, sharp knife, chopping board, lemon squeezer, basin, teaspoon, wooden spoon, sauce boat.

For success:

Stir well as the sauce thickens.

1 Pour the syrup from the jug into the saucepan.

2 Add the marmalade.

3 Cut the orange into halves and squeeze out the juice.

4 Put the cornflour into the basin and blend with the orange juice.

5 Tip this into the saucepan.

6 Light the gas burner or switch on the electric hotplate and turn the heat low.

7 Stir all the time as the sauce thickens and becomes smooth.

8 Pour into a sauce boat and serve hot or cold.

Ginger pear upside down cake

This is another excellent pudding or cake. It has pears at the bottom and a ginger-flavoured cake. On page 127 is a ginger sauce to serve with it. Upside down cakes are very popular in America.

You will need:

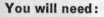

for the glaze:

margarine	25 grammes (1 oz)
golden syrup	2 tablespoons
canned pear halves	6–8

for the cake:

margarine	100 grammes (4 oz)
castor sugar	100 grammes (4 oz)
eggs	2
self-raising flour (or plain flour and 1½ level teaspoons baking powder)	150 grammes (6 oz)
ground ginger	1–2 teaspoons
milk	1 tablespoon

These ingredients will make 6–8 slices.

You will use:

plates for ingredients, flat-bladed knife, 18 cm (7 inch) cake tin (*without a loose base*) or round or square oven-proof dish, tablespoon, can opener, jug, mixing bowl, wooden spoon, cup, sieve, teaspoon, large serving plate.

123

For success:

Follow the directions for creaming on
page 153 and test the cake carefully at
stage 15. Page 154 tells you about testing
cakes.

1 Set your oven to very moderate,
325–350°F, or 170–180°C or Gas Mark 3–4.

2 Spread most of the margarine at the
bottom of the cake tin or oven-proof
dish, and a little round the sides of the
tin or dish.

3 Put the golden syrup at the bottom of
the tin.

4 Make 2 holes in the can of halved pears.
This is not an easy thing to do, so it
would be a good idea to ask a grown-up
to help you.

5 Pour all the liquid from the can into
the jug, then spoon 1 tablespoon of this
liquid over the golden syrup.

6 Open the can of pears properly and lift
out the pears.

7 Arrange 6–8 halves in a neat design
over the golden syrup and tablespoon
of liquid from the can.

8 Put the margarine and sugar into the mixing bowl.

9 Cream with the wooden spoon until soft and light (see page 153).

10 Break the first egg into a cup, then add to the margarine and sugar, and beat well.

11 Break the second egg into a cup, then add to the margarine and sugar, and beat well.

12 Sieve the flour (or flour and baking powder) and ground ginger into the mixing bowl, then blend into the margarine mixture with an ordinary tablespoon.

13 Lastly, add the milk and mix gently but thoroughly.

See the note on page 153 about how you can cream margarine and sugar very quickly if using the modern soft margarines.

14 Spoon the cake mixture on top of the pears, scrape the bowl clean, and smooth the mixture very flat on top.

15 Bake for 1½ hours in the middle of a very moderate oven until firm to the touch; page 154 tells you about testing cakes.

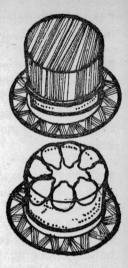

16 Take out of the oven CAREFULLY, and let it stand for 3 minutes.

17 Have the large serving plate ready and tip the cake upside down on to this.

18 Serve hot or cold, either by itself or with the ginger sauce or with ice cream.

Ginger sauce

This sauce is very good poured over ice cream as well.

You will need:

golden syrup	2 tablespoons
preserved or crystallized ginger	50 grammes (2 oz)
cornflour	2 LEVEL teaspoons
water*	good ¼ litre (284 ml) or ½ pint

*Or use the liquid from the canned pears (in the ginger pear upside down cake). As this is rather sweet use only 1 tablespoon golden syrup.

These ingredients will make 6–8 servings.

You will use:

tablespoon, saucepan, chopping board, sharp knife, basin, teaspoon, measuring jug, wooden spoon, sauce boat.

For success:

Stir well as the sauce thickens.

1 Put the golden syrup into the saucepan.

2 Put the preserved or crystallized ginger on a chopping board and cut it into small pieces, tip the ginger into the saucepan.

3 Put the cornflour into the basin and blend with the water.

4 Pour into the saucepan.

5 Light the gas burner or switch on the electric hotplate and turn the heat low.

6 Stir all the time as the sauce thickens and becomes smooth.

7 Pour into a sauce boat and serve hot or cold.

Caramelled rice pudding

The caramel topping makes this rice
pudding very interesting. If you have not
time to cook the pudding, open a can
of creamed rice, tip it into a pie dish
and warm it for about 20 minutes
in the oven, then add the sugar topping.

You will need:

For the pudding:

round (often called Carolina) rice	2 tablespoons
castor or granulated sugar	1–2 tablespoons
milk	generous ½ litre (1 pint)
butter (optional)	small knob

For the sugar topping:

brown sugar	2–3 tablespoons

These ingredients will make 4 servings.

You will use:

plates for ingredients, 1 litre (1½–2 pint)
pie dish, tablespoon, measure for milk
(although this can be poured from the
bottle or carton), flat-bladed knife.

For success:

Cook a rice pudding, or any other milk puddings you make, as slowly as possible in the oven.

1 Set your oven at slow to very slow, 275–300°F, or 140–150°C or Gas Mark 2–3.

2 Put the rice, castor or granulated sugar and milk into the pie dish. It is a good idea to add the small piece of butter, for that gives a more creamy pudding; but a piece of suet or margarine could be used instead.

3 Put the pudding into the centre of the oven and let it cook for about 2 hours, or follow the instructions given under 'To make a change' on page 131.

4 When the pudding is almost ready to serve take it out of the oven CAREFULLY; be careful where you put it down – the pie dish can crack if it is put on a damp surface.

5 Sprinkle enough brown sugar over the top to give a good coating and put the pudding back again in the oven, but place the dish nearer the top of the oven, so the sugar makes a moist brown topping.

To make a change:

It wastes heat if you use the oven just for a pudding, so you could bake *large* jacket potatoes. Page 96 tells you how to prepare these. They will take the same time as the pudding, if placed near the centre of the oven.

You can cook the rice pudding (and jacket potatoes) rather more quickly, i.e. in a moderate oven, 325–350°F, 170–180°C or Gas Mark 3–4. This means that when you make the hunter's chicken casserole (page 95), you can put the rice pudding into the oven about 30 minutes before the casserole. Cook the pudding towards the bottom of the oven.

Cherry tarts

These tarts taste as good as they look.
Make sure the pastry is baked until crisp,
and allow it and the glaze (see recipe)
to cool before you fill the tarts.

You will need:

for the pastry:

flour, preferably plain	100 grammes (4 oz)
salt	pinch
margarine or butter or cooking fat	50 grammes (2 oz)
egg yolk	1
water	nearly 1 tablespoon

for the filling:

cherries	1 medium can
red currant jelly	2 tablespoons
cornflour	1 LEVEL teaspoon

These ingredients will make 9–12 tarts.

You will use:

plates for ingredients, sieve, mixing
bowl, tablespoon, flat-bladed knife,
flour dredger, pastry board, rolling pin,
5–8 cm (2–3 inch) pastry cutter, 9 fairly
large or 12 smaller patty tins, fork, wire
cooling tray, can opener, measuring jug,
saucepan, teaspoon, basin, wooden
spoon, pastry brush (optional), serving
dish.

132

For success:

Do not make the pastry dough too damp at stage 4.
Stir the glaze carefully over a *low* heat as it thickens.

1 Do not heat the oven too early as it takes time to make pastry.

2 Sieve the flour and salt into the mixing bowl; add the margarine, butter or cooking fat.

3 Rub the fat into the flour with the tips of your fingers until the mixture looks like fine breadcrumbs; do not handle the mixture too much.

4 Add the egg yolk, then gradually add enough water to make the mixture bind together in a ball. You will find you can mix the ingredients with a flat-bladed knife, but it is better to use your finger tips to gather the dough into a ball.

5 Set your oven to hot, 425–450°F, 220–230°C or Gas Mark 6–7.

6 Shake a little flour on to the pastry board, then put the pastry dough on it.

7 Shake a little flour over the rolling pin.

8 Roll the pastry lightly, but firmly, until it makes a neat shape, about ½ cm (¼ inch) in thickness.

9 Cut out the rounds with a pastry cutter.

10 Fit these into some of the patty tins, then gather up the pieces of pastry dough and press them gently together.

11 Flour the rolling pin again, roll out the dough as in stage 8, then cut out the rest of the rounds (as in stage 9).

12 Prick the tart shapes with a fork; this stops them rising, so that they keep a good shape as they are cooked.

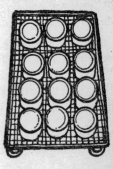

13 Bake for about 12–15 minutes in the centre of the hot oven.

14 Take the patty tins out of the oven, and let the pastry 'set' for a few minutes; this makes it less likely to break as you handle it.

15 Lift each tart case out of the patty tins very carefully and put on to a wire cooling tray.

16 Make 2 holes in the can of cherries, or ask a grown-up to do this for you.

17 Pour a generous ⅛ litre (142 ml) or ¼ pint of the liquid in the can into the measuring jug: if you have not quite enough add water to give the right quantity.

18 Now open the can completely and lift out the cherries and put them on to a plate. Make sure you do not add any of the syrup to the cherries; they need to be dry, otherwise they will spoil the crispness of the pastry.

19 Put the red currant jelly into the saucepan.

20 Put the cornflour into a basin, then gradually stir in the liquid from the can; stir all the time as you do this, so the mixture keeps smooth.

21 Tip this into the saucepan.

22 Light the gas burner or switch on the electric hotplate and turn the heat low.

23 Stir the red currant jelly mixture with the wooden spoon over the heat until it thickens and turns bright and clear.

24 Take the pan off the heat and let this mixture begin to cool – it must not be too cold, otherwise it becomes too stiff.

25 Arrange a few cherries in each tart case.

26 Either spread the red currant mixture which is called 'the glaze' over the cherries with a teaspoon or flat-bladed knife or dip the pastry brush into the glaze and brush this over the cherries. Use up all the glaze.

27 Let the glaze become quite cold, then place the tarts on a serving dish.

To make a change:

You can use other fruit instead of cherries.

A quick way of making pastry

The modern soft (often called luxury) margarines and vegetable fats soften so easily today that you can make pastry without rubbing the fat into the flour. All you need to do is to put all the ingredients for the pastry into the mixing bowl and mix together with a fork, then continue from stage 5 onwards.

Ice cream

There are many ways of preparing your own ice cream; this recipe makes a very special kind of ice cream, but it does cost quite a lot of money, so I expect you will only have it on special occasions. If you read 'To make a change' on page 139 you will see how to make the ice cream without spending quite so much money.

You will need:

eggs	2
castor or icing sugar	about 50 grammes (2 oz)
vanilla essence	few drops
thick cream	⅛ litre (142 ml) or ¼ pint
thin cream	⅛ litre (142 ml) or ¼ pint

These ingredients will make 4–6 servings.

You will use:

plates for ingredients, cup, 2 basins, sieve, wooden spoon, egg whisk, skewer, tablespoon, large freezing tray, serving dishes.

For success:

Do whisk hard at stage 3, for this makes a very light ice cream.
Do not over-beat the thick cream at stage 5.

1 Break the first egg into a cup, then tip it into a basin; break the second egg into the cup, then tip this into the basin.

2 Add the sugar; if you are using icing sugar press this through a sieve with a wooden spoon.

3 Whisk the eggs and sugar until they are thick; you may want to stop once or twice to have a rest as this is quite hard work and may take a little time.

4 Dip a skewer into the bottle of vanilla essence and let a few drops fall into the mixture; do not add too much.

5 Pour the thick cream into the second basin and whisk this until it holds its shape.

6 Pour in the thin cream and mix with the thick cream and whisk again until the mixture stands up in points.

7 Spoon the cream into the beaten eggs and sugar, taste the ice cream and add a little more vanilla essence if necessary.

8 Spoon it into the freezing tray and freeze it as quickly as possible in the freezing compartment of the refrigerator, or put it into the deep freeze. It will take at least 1–1½ hours to freeze.

9 Spoon into the serving dishes.

To make a change :

Chocolate ice cream : Add 1 level
tablespoon sieved cocoa or 2
tablespoons chocolate powder at stage
4; you can still use the vanilla essence.

Coffee ice cream : Mix 1 teaspoon instant
coffee powder with 1 tablespoon milk
and add to the mixture at stage 4; you
do not need the vanilla essence.

Fruit ice cream : Rub ¼ kilo (8 oz)
strawberries or raspberries through a
sieve or mash them with a fork. Add to
the ice cream at stage 4; you do not
need the vanilla essence.

Cheaper ice cream : Use ¼ litre (284 ml) or
½ pint unsweetened evaporated milk
instead of the thick and thin cream.
Whip this until it is fluffy then use
instead of the cream at stage 7.

Custard ice cream : Make a thick custard
(see the recipe for trifle on page 142)
with only 1 tablespoon custard powder,
¼ litre (284 ml) or ½ pint milk. Add 50
grammes (2 oz) castor or sieved icing
sugar to the custard. *Cover* with damp
greaseproof paper, so a skin does not
form and allow the custard to cool. Add
the custard to the whipped cream or
whipped evaporated milk and freeze.

Fudge walnut sauce

You will need:

vanilla fudge	100 grammes (4 oz)
top of the milk or	
thin cream	2 tablespoons
halved walnuts	25–50 grammes (1–2 oz)

These ingredients will make 4–6 servings.

You will use:

double saucepan or basin and saucepan, tablespoon, chopping board, sharp knife, wooden spoon.

For success:

Do not over-heat the fudge.

1 Put the fudge with the top of the milk or thin cream into the top of the double saucepan or into a basin which fits S A F E L Y over the saucepan.

2 Put cold water into the bottom of the double saucepan or saucepan.

3 Light the gas burner or switch on the electric hotplate; turn to moderate.

4 Leave the fudge mixture until it melts, then turn off the heat.

5 Lift the top off the double saucepan or lift the basin out of the water, or ask a grown-up to do this for you, for it must be done CAREFULLY.

6 Put the walnuts on to the chopping board, and cut them into smaller pieces.

7 Add these to the melted fudge and stir well; the sauce can be used hot or cold. If you are using the sauce hot do not pour over the ice cream until the very last minute.

Ways to serve ice cream

Ice cream can be served in many ways:

Top individual portions of jelly with ice cream.

Serve ice cream with raw, cooked or canned fruit.

Top ice cream with a sauce.
Page 121 gives an orange sauce and page 127 gives a ginger sauce.

There is a chocolate sauce in the first *Piccolo Cook Book* and a fudge walnut sauce on the opposite page.

Trifle

You will need:

trifle sponge cakes 3–4
jam   3 tablespoons

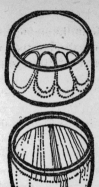

for the custard sauce:
custard powder   2 tablespoons
castor or
granulated sugar   2 tablespoons
milk   good ½ litre (1 pint)

for decoration:
thick cream   3–4 tablespoons
glacé cherries   about 6
angelica   tiny pieces

These ingredients will make 4–6 servings.

You will use:

plates for ingredients, tablespoon,
flat-bladed knife, serving dish, basin,
saucepan, wooden spoon, egg whisk,
teaspoon, sharp knife.

For success:

Stir the custard as it thickens to make
sure it keeps smooth.

DO NOT POUR TOO HOT
CUSTARD OVER THE SPONGE
CAKES otherwise you may crack the
dish.

1 Split the sponge cakes through the centre and spread with the jam, then sandwich them together again.

2 Put them into the serving dish.

3 Put the custard powder and sugar into the basin, and blend with a little of the milk.

4 Pour the rest of the milk into the saucepan.

5 Light the gas burner or switch on the electric hotplate and heat the milk; watch carefully to see it does not boil over.

6 Pour the very hot milk over the custard, stirring well as you do so.

7 Tip the custard mixture back into the saucepan. Put it back on the burner or hotplate, keeping the heat fairly low.

8 Stir with the wooden spoon as the custard thickens and cook SLOWLY for about 5 minutes after it thickens.

9 Allow the custard to cool slightly, stirring once or twice to stop a skin forming.

10 Pour the warm custard over the sponge cakes, then cover the serving dish with a plate and allow the custard to cool.

11 Pour the cream into a basin and whip until it becomes thick.

12 Put small teaspoons of cream on top of the custard and decorate with halved glacé cherries and tiny pieces of angelica.

To make a change:

Fruit trifle

1 Ingredients as for the trifle on page 142, but you also need a small can of mixed fruit salad.

2 Open the can of fruit and pour the syrup from the can over the sponge cakes at stage 2.

3 Tip the fruit on to a plate and cut it into smaller pieces.

4 Spoon over the sponge cakes, then finish making the trifle as in stages 3–12.

Sherry trifle

1 Ingredients as for the trifle on page 142, but add 3 tablespoons sweet sherry.

2 Spoon the sherry over the top, then finish making the trifle as in stages 3–12.

Compôte of fruit

This is the name given to fruit when it is cooked; it is often called stewed fruit.

If the fruit is hard, like plums, you will need $\frac{1}{4}$ litre (284 ml) or $\frac{1}{2}$ pint water and 50–75 grammes (2–3 oz) sugar to each $\frac{1}{2}$ kilo (1 lb) fruit.

If the fruit is soft, like blackcurrants or raspberries, you will need only $\frac{1}{8}$ litre (142 ml) or $\frac{1}{4}$ pint water and 50-75 grammes (2-3 oz) sugar to each $\frac{1}{2}$ kilo (1 lb) fruit.

Put the water and sugar into a saucepan and heat it until the sugar has melted. Add the prepared fruit (e.g. peeled and sliced apples or halved stoned large plums). Simmer gently until the fruit is tender.

If you are using the oven on a low heat you can put the water, sugar and fruit into a casserole, cover it with a lid and cook for about 40 minutes until the fruit is tender.

Fruit salad

The first *Piccolo Cook Book* gives one recipe for fruit salad; another way to prepare this is to cook a mixture of fruits in a compôte.

Orange Alaska

This dessert is quite a surprise; you have the hot meringue on top of firm cold ice cream. Do time the cooking carefully though, for meringue burns easily in a very hot oven but, if you have a cooler oven heat, the ice cream will melt.

You will need:

oranges	2 very large
castor sugar	65 grammes (2½ oz)
egg whites	2
ice cream	4 tablespoons

These ingredients will make 4 servings.

You will use:

chopping board, sharp knife, teaspoon, basin, plate for sugar, mixing bowl or second basin, egg whisk, large plate, tablespoon, oven-proof dish or plate or tin with a serving plate.

For success:

Make sure the egg whites are very stiff and the meringue covers the ice cream.

1 Set your oven to very hot, 475°F, or 240°C or Gas Mark 8–9.

2 Cut the oranges in halves across the centre. Remove the pulp with the teaspoon and put into a basin.

3 Sweeten with 15 grammes ($\frac{1}{2}$ oz) of the sugar and put back into the halved orange cases.

4 Start to whisk the egg whites (see tips on page 99 for separating egg whites and whisking them) until nearly stiff, and cover the bowl with a plate so they do not become liquid again.

5 Put the ice cream on top of the orange pulp.

6 Continue whisking the egg whites until they are very stiff.

7 Whisk in half the sugar, fold in the remainder.

8 Spoon on top of the ice cream and stand on an oven-proof dish or plate or tin.

9 Bake for about 3 minutes only in the centre of a very hot oven.

10 Serve as quickly as possible on the dish or plate on which the meringue was baked or lift from the tin on to a serving plate.

Lemon and banana flan

This flan uses biscuit crumbs and a
very delicious lemon and banana
mixture. It would be splendid for a special
party. It does not need cooking, but you
must start making it in good time so that
the jelly will set.

You will need:

lemon jelly	1 packet
water	good ¼ litre (284 ml) or ½ pint
thick cream	⅛ litre (142 ml) or ¼ pint
lemon	1
bananas	3
sugar	1 tablespoon

for the flan case:

digestive biscuits	150 grammes (6 oz)
butter or margarine	75 grammes (3 oz)
castor sugar	50 grammes (2 oz)

These ingredients will make 6 servings.

You will use:

plates for ingredients, 3 basins (1 must
be heat resisting), kettle, heat resisting
measuring jug, wooden spoon, egg whisk,
sharp knife, chopping board, lemon
squeezer, fork, tablespoon, greaseproof
paper, rolling pin, serving plate,
flan ring (not essential), teaspoon.

For success:

Make quite sure the jelly is beginning to set before you add the cream and mashed bananas.

1 Separate the pieces of the jelly tablet and put into the heat resisting basin.

2 Put the water in the kettle and either light the gas burner or switch on the electric hotplate or electric kettle.

3 Let the water come to boiling point, then pour it (or ask a grown-up to do this) into the measuring jug to give the right amount.

4 Pour the water over the jelly and stir with a wooden spoon until dissolved.

5 Allow the jelly to cool, then put it in the refrigerator and leave it until it *begins to stiffen slightly*. This will take at least 1½–2 hours; do not let it become too stiff.

6 Pour the cream into a basin and whisk it until it just stands up in peaks.

7 Cut the lemon in half and squeeze out the juice.

8 Put the bananas into the third basin and mash them with a fork, then add the sugar and the lemon juice; mix well together.

9 Fold the mashed bananas and then *half* the cream into the partly set jelly. Put the basin containing the rest of the cream in a cool place. You need this for the decoration.

10 Put the jelly mixture back in the refrigerator for a short time to become stiffer.

11 Meanwhile prepare the flan case.

12 Put the digestive biscuits on to a sheet of greaseproof paper.

13 Cover with a second sheet of paper and roll gently but firmly with the rolling pin until you make fine crumbs; leave on the paper for the time being.

14 Put the butter or margarine and sugar into a basin and cream with a wooden spoon until soft.

15 Gradually add the crumbs and stir well (you may find a metal tablespoon easier and better than the wooden spoon).

16 Form the biscuit mixture into a flan shape, as in the picture. This means making a flat round for the base, then a rim of about 2½ cm (1 inch) all round. If you have a plain 20 cm (8 inch) flan ring you can put this on the serving plate and make the flan shape in it then lift it away very carefully.

17 Put the flan in a cool place to set – this will take about ½ hour. At the same time make sure the jelly mixture is not becoming too firm.

18 Spoon the jelly mixture into the flan case.

19 Top with the rest of the whipped cream.

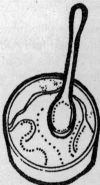

To make a change:
Instead of the lemon and banana mixture, you can use an orange filling – see page 152.

Orange flan

Use an orange jelly instead of the lemon jelly; you do not need the lemon. Use a small can of mandarin oranges instead of the bananas.

1 Dissolve the orange jelly in the good $\frac{1}{4}$ litre (284 ml) or $\frac{1}{2}$ pint water as described in stages 1–4 on page 149.

2 Open the can of mandarin oranges and add a good $\frac{1}{8}$ litre (142 ml) or $\frac{1}{4}$ pint of the liquid from the can, then drain the oranges from the can through a sieve and add these to the jelly.

3 Allow the jelly mixture to stiffen slightly, then fold *half* the whipped cream into this, as in stage 9, and continue to the end of the recipe.

Did you know?

Creaming margarine and sugar in recipes is quite hard work; you will make it easier if:

1 You choose the modern soft (luxury) margarines or vegetable fats.

These are so soft that you do not need to work hard at all.

In fact you can put all the ingredients of the cake recipe (for example, orange upside down cake) into a mixing bowl and cream them together; this saves a a great deal of time.

2 Always stand the mixing bowl on a teacloth, this will save it slipping as you beat the mixture with a wooden spoon.

3 Use a teacloth under the mixing bowl when you whisk egg whites.

If you keep eggs in the refrigerator take them out 1 hour before separating and whisking; if egg whites are too cold they will not whisk well.

Testing cakes

1 See if the cake has shrunk away from the sides of the tin.

2 Press firmly on top. If your finger leaves a mark the cake is not done.

3 Tip the tin carefully over the wire cooling tray or plate. A grown-up should help you do this.

Did you know?

The best way to line cake tins with paper is as follows:

1 Cut a round or square the size of the base of the tin – to do this put the tin over the paper and draw round it.

2 Put this on one side while you prepare the paper for the sides of the tin.
Fold the paper to give a double band round the inside of the tin. Make slits about 1 cm ($\frac{1}{2}$ inch) deep at 1 cm ($\frac{1}{2}$ inch) intervals along one side of the paper.

3 Put this into the cake tin and fold the bottom part so the slits 'spread out' and give a neat fit at the bottom edge of the tin.

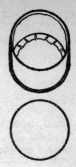

4 Put the round or square on top of this.

Did you know?

There are two ways of greasing cake tins or the paper-lined cake tins:

1 Melt a little fat in a saucepan or old basin standing in hot water. Dip a pastry brush in the melted fat and brush round the bottom and sides of the tin.
Instead of melted fat you could use oil.

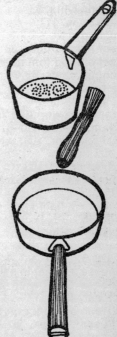

2 Do not melt the fat.
Take a small piece of greaseproof paper. Put a very little fat on this and rub it round the bottom and sides of the tin.

To look after frying pans:

Either wash them well after use and dry well or take a piece of soft kitchen paper and wipe round the inside of the pan, as soon as you have used it and it has had time to become cool. You can wash the outside, but if you wipe out the inside the food is less likely to stick.

INDEX

156

Piccolo Non-Fiction

Have you sampled Marguerite Patten's first book written especially for junior cooks? It's as jam-packed with delicious ideas and useful advice as this one – and as easy to follow.

PICCOLO COOK BOOK (illus)   25p

If you'd rather just concentrate on the sweeter things in life, then you'll find this book irresistible!

Margaret Powell
SWEETMAKING FOR CHILDREN
  (illus)   20p

Toffee ... fudge ... marzipan ... nothing tastes as good as real home-made sweets! Join in the (delicious!) fun as Margaret Powell explains in this amusing and practical guide how everything's done, from choosing the utensils to decorating the finished goodies – not forgetting, of course, her five golden rules for safety in the kitchen. Her easy-to-follow recipes show you how to make all kinds of mouth-watering sweets, from peppermint creams that need no cooking, to fancy chocolates for a special present.

More Piccolo
Non-Fiction

Elizabeth Gundrey
SEWING THINGS (illus)   25p

Whether you've tried sewing anything before
or not, these simple, step-by-step instructions,
fully illustrated, will tell you all you need to
know, from choosing the patterns, colours and
materials, to decorating your finished article.
There are dozens of good ideas here for things
to make, presents for the whole family and
things for the home, and of course exciting and
original clothes for yourself – anything from a
happi-coat to an Afro-tunic!

GROWING THINGS (illus)   25p

Have fun growing things even if you haven't
got a real garden! With plenty of clear diagrams
to help you, this book explains all the different
ways to grow fascinating plants, and how to
look after them whether your garden is in a
bottle, in a hanging basket, or even underwater.
And whether it's a miniature tree from a fruit
stone, a plant from a turnip, or something
more exotic, you'll be amazed at what you can
grow!

These and other PICCOLO Books are obtain-
able from all booksellers and newsagents. If you
have any difficulty please send purchase price
plus 7p postage to PO Box 11, Falmouth,
Cornwall.
While every effort is made to keep prices low, it
is sometimes necessary to increase prices at
short notice. PAN Books reserve the right to
show new retail prices on covers which may
differ from those advertised in the text or
elsewhere.